Needle Felting Book for Beginners

Craft Amazing Needle Felting Patterns, and Needle Felted Animals and Projects with Wool Using this Step by Step User Instructions Guide (Pictures Included)

By

Angela Kemp

Disclaimer

This publication is designed to provide competent and reliable information regarding the subject matter covered. However, the views expressed in this publication are those of the author alone, and should not be taken as expert instruction or professional advice. The reader is responsible for his or her own actions.

The author hereby disclaims any responsibility or liability whatsoever that is incurred from the use or application of the contents of this publication by the purchaser or reader. The purchaser or reader is hereby responsible for his or her own actions.

Table of Contents

Introduction

Do you need a skill that will improve your coordination ability?

Do you want to learn an easy craft within the shortest time?

Do you want to improve your creative ability?

Do you want to improve your felting skills?

Do you need an alternative source of income?

If this is you, then you are in the right place. I will take your hands and walk you through this fantastic craft called needle felting and help you learn all you need to know about the craft to start making unique designs in no time.

I wrote this book with you in mind to give a detailed non-fluffy step-by-step tutorial on how to learn needle felting and start creating fantastic crafts.

Are you wondering why you should learn needle felting?

Here are your answers:

- Needle felting is credited with becoming a popular form of stress relief, as the repeated motions of the needle can be very therapeutic.
- Needle felting is a means of improving the brain's functions and reducing Alzheimer's disease.
- Needle felting is calming.
- It is less expensive than other crafts.
- It can fetch you a good amount of money

…And lots more.

This book has great value for you no matter the stage you are in needle felting. If you are a beginner, this book will provide the right information you need to get you started with your first needle felting craft. If you want to improve your craft, this book can help you step up your skills and introduce you to new projects. If you are a pro, you can also pick some new knowledge to add to your existing knowledge.

This book's structure begins by giving a short introduction into what needle felting is all about, how it emanated, reasons to indulge in the craft, important terminologies to be aware of, and then goes further to list the tools and materials you need for needle felting. Most importantly, it gives a detailed step by step guide of 15 needle felting projects around animals and inanimate objects that you can start creating immediately from the comfort of your home. The last chapter addresses all the questions you can possibly think of regarding needle felting. There is just a whole lot of great stuff for you in this book.

I can assure you that if you read through this book and apply all that I have written for you, you will become an expert needle felter in no time. This book is not a book you read once. It is registered as a guide. So, read it as much as you can until you become well versed in the art of needle felting.

Read.
Learn.
Apply.
Become a PRO.
And start creating some magical crafts!

Chapter 1

What is Needle Felting?

Have you ever stared amazingly at needle felting designs and wondered if you could embark on such an enormous project?

Do you want to learn the intricacies of needle felting, but yet, you feel overwhelmed even to get started?

My answer is this:

"Yes, you can learn how needle felting works to create amazing works of art!"

Needle felting is not rocket science; you can learn it with the right learning guide and practice.

That is why I created this book with you in mind, to give you a head start in your quest and give you a step-to-step guide to learn needle felting and craft out awesome designs in no time. It is written in a non-fluffy, straight to the point manner to aid your learning process and set you on the way to creating great felted designs.

So, let's delve into the basics of Needle Felting.

To begin with, Needle Felting is simply the process of turning wool into 3D with the use of a barbed needle. It involves agitating the fibers of wool so that they fuse in a stiff form. If you have ever knitted before, this process is likely familiar. However, a significant difference is that while other felting processes involve using hot water to make the fibers bond, needle felting instead uses a very sharp needle.

Needle felting involves piercing a needle repeatedly inside a piece of loose wool (also called wool roving) to make it stiff and get it into a solid, three-dimensional shape. The needle barbs make the fibers intertwine with one another, making the wool to maintain its shape when finished.

Needle felting sounds simple in concept, but it can be an elaborate process to execute. In the end, you create 3D sculptures from wool.

Most needle felting sculptures are animal-like due to their fuzziness, which is excellent for the wool's fibers' fuzziness. However, you can make anything with needle felting, ranging from people, animals, food, and even imaginary creatures.

Needle felting is not like sewing. It is more like a wool sculpting. Here, you form a shape by adding more wool as you continue until you are cool with the results. Needle felting also includes a lot of repetitive movements, but it doesn't require your full attention. However, it would help if you were careful to avoid stabbing yourself with the felting needle.

History of Needle Felting

Felting, which involves interlocking or matting wool fibers, is one of the first forms of creating textiles. It did not include spinning or weaving to produce fabric from wool. It only involved compacting fibers to have a tangible creation.

Unlike the history of wet felting, which is popular and has many exciting stories woven around it, the history of needle felting is unpopular.

Needle felting started in the 1800s, with the needle punch machine getting its first patent in 1859. The needle punch machines were used to make insulation and batting from slaughterhouse fibers, torn woolen garments, and even soldier's haircuts. Industrially, they used needle felting to make felted fabric without using soap and water solution. The felting mills also felt various uses like dust barriers, gaskets, carpet pads, and latterly for industries that produce car carpets. The humble tennis ball is a famous needle felted product with elaborate needled felted covering with a particular aerodynamic characteristic.

However, needle felting became established in the 1980s when Eleanor and David Stanwood moved to Martha's Vineyard from Sonoma County. They worked with some felt makers from Belgium who were owners of a few textile mills. David and Eleanor wanted to create small pieces of felt without soap or water. They brought home needles from the wool factory and used them to create felt in a little way. Eleanor was creative, and she went ahead to develop quilts for wraps and scarves from this felting method. Later, a Californian textile artist called Ayala Tapai got information about the felting needs and tried it out in her kitchen. From Ayala, the attention got spread to Birgitte Krag Hansent, a Danish felt artist; who had been using the wet felting method. She became interested in the needle felting method, and soon the craft started spreading across

Scandinavia. From that country, the art crossed the North Sea to the United Kingdom.

Currently, needle felting has gained massive popularity in various nations of the world.

How Does Needle Felting Work?

Needle felting works by using special needles called felting needles that have tiny barbs at their bottom. These needles are of various shapes like triangular or star-shaped, and the barbs are cut out around the corners of the needles.

What happens is that when you pierce the needle into the wool, the barbs will grab the strands of wool and drag them down but not back up again. So, when you pierce the needle into the wool repeatedly, the wool will become entangled on itself. Wool possesses tiny scales on the fiber shaft that sticks them together when they are tangled. The more the piercing of the felting needle on the wool, the firmer and more entangled the wool becomes, making it tight and heavier.

Other Forms of Felting

Apart from needle felting, there are other forms of felting, such as wet felting.

Felting is defined as the process of matting, condensing, and pressing fibers together. You can felt natural fibers like animal fur or wool or synthetic fibers like acrylonitrile, wood pulp-based rayon, and petroleum-based acrylic. You can also blend fibers. Felting can be used in various industries and manufacturing processes like the automotive industry, casinos, musical instruments, home construction, and gun wadding either in cartridges or pushed down a muzzleloader's barrel.

Wet Felting

Wet felting involves applying hot water to layers of animal hairs and then agitating and compressing them to make the fibers hook together or weave together to a single piece of fabric. To improve the process's speed, wrap the arranged wool in a sturdy, textured material like the bamboo mat or burlap. You can also finish the felting by filling.

Only a specific type of fibers can be wet felted. Examples are most types of fleece, especially those from alpaca or Merino sheep. Also, mohair (goat), angora (rabbit), or hair from rodents like beavers and muskrats.

Difference Between Wet Felting and Needle Felting
The significant difference between wet felting and needle felting is that wet felting uses hot water, soap, and agitation to tangle the fibers into felt. In contrast, needle felting uses a needle felting tool's up and down movement to create friction to form felt.

However, both processes are irreversible. Once a fiber becomes felt, it remains felt.

Reasons to Indulge in Needle Felting

If you wonder if there are any intrinsic and external benefits to needle felting, your answer is just right here. Here are some of the reasons for you to indulge in needle felting:

It is less expensive: The materials needed for needle felting are relatively cheap. You only need a needle or multiple needles, wool, and sponge or foam block as a working platform. It would be best if you used the foam/sponge block to protect the needle from breaking.

Wool roving is also cheap. When compared to the products of your knitting, the materials are not expensive.

It is more straightforward than other crafts: Needle felting might not be very easy, but when compared to other knitting and crocheting process, needle felting is easy and less complicated. Here, you don't need to memorize loops, do stitches, or follow patterns except you desire to. However, the only challenge is that needle felting can be time-consuming. A straightforward project can take close to two hours, and an elaborate piece can consume days and even weeks. You can increase the project's speed with a felting pen that can hold three needles instead of one needle.

Needle felting is calming: If you want to seek ways to relax your mind and unwind, needle felting is a great way to go about this. It helps your mind to remain focused and calm, which can provide therapeutic benefits.

4. **Needle felting helps you create virtually anything:** With needle felting, you can create almost anything you desire. Even though it is a part of fiber arts, it is related to molding with clay. Many people

create little figures of animals and toys, others create huge models, while others create abstract art. You have the full freedom to create what you desire.

Needle felting can reduce your chances of having Alzheimer's disease: Research by Mayo's clinic has shown that involving yourself in a craft like a needle felting can reduce your risk of getting Alzheimer's by 30 to 50%. When you learn this skill, you are giving your brain a needed exercise. Also, hand-eye coordination is an essential skill in learning needle felting, and that skill can help protect your brain against Alzheimer's.

Needle felting can fetch you some income: You can earn some good cash from needle felting. You can sell, work on commission, create and sell your kits, organize tutorials, and create online courses on the subject.

Ways You Can Earn From Needle Felting

There are several ways that you can earn from needle felting, and they include:

Selling your crafts: You can your felted objects in various places both online and offline

Creating and selling your kits for others to make things: You can design and create kits for people to buy to give your business another dimension.

Work on Commission: Instead of creating lots of things, you can get commissioned work. This way, you will know that you will sell the item and not spend time on things that may not sell or may not sell for a while.

Online Tutorials: You can create online courses that will give people the information that they need concerning needle felting at a reasonable price.

Books or Ebooks: You can write ebooks on needle felting and enlighten people on the subject at a price.

Offline Courses: You can also organize and run a course locally. From there, you can sell wool, books, and equipment to your students.

Places to Sell Your Felted Projects, Books, and Kits

If you are wondering where you can sell your needle felted projects, I have you covered. The top sites that you can sell them are as follows:

Etsy: This is currently the number one place to sell your craft online, whether needle felting or other crafts. A lot of crafters sell mostly on Etsy.

However, using Etsy alone can limit your sales. The reason is there are a lot of people selling different things. Therefore, your chances of standing out are not that high. It would help if you branded yourself differently from Etsy to draw customers to Etsy to sell your wares. To carry that out, you need other channels.

Your Website: You can create your website and use it to market your services. You can also sell your felted materials to sell your craft.

Facebook: This is another avenue where you can sell your craft. You can join Facebook communities where people sell their crafts or use your Facebook page to sell your skills.

Amazon: You can also consider using Amazon to sell your crafts.

Craft Fairs: Craft fairs are other great locations to sell your crafts. When you go to craft fairs, give out your cards to people, and get people to know you.

Local Craft Shops or Marketplaces: You can also put your crafts for sale in local shops. A lot of people have tried this. Go for big stores and outlets that have a broad coverage of customers. That way, you will be able to make sales.

Chapter 2

Basic Needle Felting Terminology

Now that you have learned the definition, uses, and history of needle felting, the next point is to know the basic terms associated with needle felting. The terminology can seem confusing, even to expert needle felters. However, this book's section will help you better understand these terms and their functions.

Needle Felting: This involves using needles with notches at the edge to make piercings into a piece or pieces of wool repeatedly. You can entangle the fibers till the wool is stiff. From there, you can assemble flat or 3D pictures, jewelry, sculptures, and others.

Wet Felting: This is the more conventional process that involves a loose pile of wool fibers, water, soap, and friction to bind the wool together and to shock the cloth to shrink and strengthen.

Micron: This refers to the measure of the thickness of wool. The lower the micron is, the better the wool. For example, Merino's thickness is usually 23 microns, but it can be as.fine as 18 microns. It would help if you went for a thicker fiber for needling felting to prevent visible needle marks from showing up on your work.

Fiber: This refers to wool or any other material that you are felting

Raw Fleece: This is gotten from the back of sheep. Then, it undergoes the arduous process of repeated washing, processing, and dyeing (when required).

Wool Tops: It is what you will be mostly using for your needle felting projects. However, it is often called roving because the two terms are frequently confused for the other. Wool tops are wool that has undergone washing and combining, with the fibers in one direction. Wool tops are usually long and are wrapped into a ball, and have about the same thickness as your wrist. There are several ranges of dyed and natural colors from which you can select. The wool top tends to separate when you gently pull them separately. But if you pull hard, the fibers will entangle together. They have tiny scales that lock together, so they are ideal for dry or wet felting.

Roving: This is a rougher version of wool tops. It is longer, thinner, loosely carded, and does not go the same direction. It does not give a smooth finish and will have pieces of vegetable matter in the wool. However, it is a nice needle felting wool that will give a rougher finish. It is also good for working with a wire armature.

Carded Batts: This refers to wool that has undergone washing and was then carded with a machine or a hand carder, which looks like a big round hairbrush; that mixes the fibers so that it runs in many directions and gives rise to shorter fibers. Batts emerge as long, springy sheets. They are typically bigger than a roving.

Core Wool: This refers to less expensive wool used for a lot of the middle of larger 3D needle felting works. Then, you can use your best wool for the top layers. A lot of people use polyester toy filling as their core.

Pre-felted Sheets: This refers to wool fibers that are only felted until they become matted but are not yet shrunk. They are then rinsed, left to dry, and then used as a starting point for a design, mostly pictures. You can either buy pre-felted sheets or make one yourself. They are thicker and more fluffy than normal felt.

Staple: The wool's length depends on the sheep it has come from and can be long or short.

Cob Web Felt: This refers to thin and soft felt that is strong enough to bind together. On the surface, cobweb felt looks like other felts. However, when it is held up against the light, it looks ethereal. It is a very transparent felt that has a holey texture.

Cobweb Felting: This is a process that gives rise to a wool felt fabric that has a cobwebby texture. A cobweb felted scarf is light and airy with thin areas and even holes.

Blends: This refers to a combination of diverse fibers and colors. Blends can produce an interesting color combination or wool that combines different fibers' characteristics.

Neeps: These are small, bobby bits of waste wool that are used to create texture.

Gauge: This refers to the width of the needle used for needle-felting. As the gauge increases, the thinner the needle gets.

Drum Carders: This is a wool-carding tool used for carding more wool than a hand carder.

Carded Fibre: This refers to fibers that have been brushed to move in multiple directions. They typically come in batts or rolags. Carded wool can be made either using large commercial felting machines, drum carders, or hand carders.

Felt: This refers to fabric produced from wool through friction, heat, and moisture, without sticking, weaving, or stitching.

Fiber: This is wool or any other material you use for felting; it is different from yarn or raw fleece. It represents the prevalence of non-sheep-wool materials such as alpaca, angora (rabbit), mohair, or natural materials such as hemp or milk tops.

Hand Carders: They are squarish, flat brushes used to carry out hand carding. They look a little like dog brushes. Dog brushes can serve as a cheaper alternative for hand carders.

Lanolin: Thes are grease found naturally in many breeds of sheep. However, alpaca fleece does not have lanolin.

Locks: These are washed curls that can be left natural or dyed. They are used for adding detail and texture.

Nepps: Little bits of waste wool that are used for creating texture.

Nuno Felt: The combination of loose fiber, like wool with a transparent textile, like silk, creating a light felt fabric. It was first created in the early 90s by Polly Sterling from Australia, and the name is gotten from the Japanese word 'Nuno,' which means cloth.

Nuno Felting: This technique combines an open weave fabric with loose fiber to produce a lightweight felt. Wool fibers work through the woven fabric before felting occurs, then when the wool shrives, the silk crinkles, creating interesting textures and shapes. You have to remember that cool water and massaging has to be done to make the wool fibers to move through the fabric. When this does not happen, the wool fibers will entangle and fall off the fabric.

Raw Wool: This is another name for fleece. It is usually unwashed and gotten straight from the back of sheep. Sheep grow wool on their body the same way human beings grow hair. Sheep also produce new fleece each year, making it a renewable fiber source.

Resist: This refers to any material placed between two sheets or pieces of wool to prevent them from felting together. These resists can be taken away at the end or around the end of the felting process.

Rolag: This refers to hard-carded batts, and are usually small in size.

Sibori: This refers to the Japanese art of pleating and knotting, and it is usually used for dyeing fabric. These techniques are used as a resist to get impressive results when you are using different color fibers.

Staple: This refers to the length of the wool fiber. It can be either long or short.

Handle: This refers to the texture of a fiber. For example: silky or harsh.

Locks: This refers to washed and dyed but unbrushed curls in their original form.

Merino: This refers to a breed of sheep that is renowned for its very soft wool. There are some issues about its use because of mulesing, which is done in some countries. Nevertheless, you can get this fiber ethically (from flocks that mulesing is not done), and some states are scrapping it.

Mulesing: This is a strategy used to stop avert flystrike. It includes removing strips of wool-bearing from around the sheep's rump to deter flies attracted by urine and feces.

Armature: This refers to a skeletal framework, typically produced from pipe cleaners or wire, that serves as the base of a sculpture and is felted around. This method is useful in creating posable models or delicate body parts like legs or thin tails.

Cria: Baby alpacas.

Noil: The short fibers that are remains from silk or wool production. They are often dyed in a similar form to a handkerchief. They are less rigid than felt but are used for texture and decoration.

Silver: This is a thinner type of roving. It is not usually used in needle felting but is mostly used in spinning.

Rolag: This is hand-carded batts of fiber that are mostly small in size and usually don't assume the shape of a small roll of fibers.

Rope: This refers to the way that fibers like tops and roving are held together.

These are the basic terms that are associated with needle felting. As you move further to the next chapters, you will encounter these terms. Therefore, have a grasp of them to understand when and how they are used in the following chapters.

Chapter 3

Top Needle Felting Tips and Tricks

If you want to produce beautiful crafts using needle felting, you need to be aware of the essential needle felting tips and tricks. These tips will guide you as you embark on your journey in creating beautiful needle felted crafts effortlessly.

The tips will be divided based on different aspects of needle felting. They include tips you should note before you start and information on the needle, felting, and finishing process.

Tips to Note Before Needle Felting

- Remember that no two sculptures are the same because you are felting with your hands and not with a machine. Therefore, making changes is allowed. Feel free to make your creations your own by adding your touch of uniqueness and having fun as you go about it. Even if you make mistakes as you create, you revisit such mistakes by gently tugging at the wool using a standard dress pin and going at it again.

- Be patient and enjoy your felting journey. You need to take your time and always remember that the detail is of great importance. Therefore, give attention to the finishing. Do not hurry the process. Take your time to select your finishing touches. You can make it as straightforward or as detailed as you desire.

- Roll the body parts tightly before you start to felt. This activity will reduce your felting time.

- Remember that needle felting is a short stabbing movement into your wool that entangles and locks the fibers. Therefore your needle should pierce only the top of the foam.

- Keep aside some wool of different colors before you commence a project. You can use the wool for correcting any mistakes or for improving your entire project.

Tips for 3D Needle Felting

- Firmness is essential to successful 3D needle felting. Ensure that your felting is firm, not hard, and can still spring back when it is squashed.

- The technique for creating 3-D felted objects is similar to that of flat needle felting. However, you to be extra careful with your fingers because it involves holding and turning your projects, and there is a bigger chance of stabbing through the wool to your finger. To avoid this, use the foam pad wherever it is possible. You can create the different parts separately, like the leg, head, hands, body, among others. Therefore, after making them, you can connect them to the main base of your figure. For instance, if you want to attach the head, place it where you desire it to be, and then stab the needle through the head entirely to the body's wool. If you do this repeatedly and through different angles, ultimately, the two pieces will be joined. Glue is not required for this.

- Ensure that you turn when felting any 3D body part to give your structure its shape and avoid dents in your shapes.

- Begin with less wool than you need. As you continue, you can add more wool to make your shape bigger; however, you cannot take away wool.

- Remember that the 3D body parts will be close to 30% smaller than the shape you began with after felting.

- Move your needle at a straight angle, up and down and not at an angle that could break your needle.

- Please, keep your hands out of harms' way as you felt. If you stab them, it will surely hurt. Therefore, be very careful.

- To create small pieces, rub the wool between your hands like dough to make a ball. It will help to tangle the fibers slightly and give you an edge on felting.

- To create medium and large pieces, it is easier to place the wool inside a smooth sheet to smooth out bumps later.

- To save wool, you can fill giant needle felted pieces with a ball of acrylic stuffing or polyfill. To do this, you can felt the acrylic stuffing first into a solid mass; then, you cover it up entirely with a layer of wool. Another strategy is to wrap sewing thread round the polyfill and cover it up with felting wool. It is a good strategy for the round, large pieces.

- Ensure that you keep backup needles when working on a project in case your needle breaks as you work on your project.

- When you start, the wool will be soft and fluffy. Within five to minutes of continuous poking, the wool will begin to take shape and become dense like a cotton ball. As you continue to poke the wool, more crosslinks will develop, and your wool will become thicker. However, this takes some time. You need to be patient.

- Know your wool. There are different kinds of wool, such as Angora, Cashmere, Merino, and Mohair. Therefore, before you engage in crafting, you need to ensure your wool is of the right quality. If you don't know where to start, you should buy a kit. Needle felting kits have everything you require to finish your project and are suitable for beginners.

- To create specific flat shapes, such as triangle, heart, or circle, you should use a cookie cutter or stencil for molding and shaping your piece. You can stuff the stencil full of wool, and place it flat on your mat, and then begin to poke. Then, flip your stencil with your wool over and then stab on the other side. Continue stabbing and turning your piece around till it becomes firm and takes on the shape of your stencil. Continue to firm the edges and fine-tune your work.

Tips on How to Use Felting Needle

- Always keep your eyes on the needle as you felt. The ends of the felting needles are sharp, and you can harm yourself.

- Hold the needle vertically to your working surface to avoid needle breakage. The needle works better when you hold it vertically. Also, to avoid needle breakage, ensure that you pull the needle out the same direction you stuck it in. Likewise, poke it straight up and down, do not tilt the needle when it is still inside the wool.

- Keep the needles back into the plastic sleeves and bag they came in after use.

- Do not keep your felting needles on wet wool. It could lead to rusting.

- Work on a firm table that has good lighting. Curling up on a couch with wool and sharp felting needles can be dangerous.

- For your work surface, use a felting pad to work. You might be tempted to hold your project in your hand during needle felting. However, it can lead to needle breakage and injury. It is better to allow the dense poly foam to absorb the felting needle's stabs and keep the project stable and bounce-free. Also, avoid thick upholstery because they make your work bouncy and lead to needle breakage and accident. Focusing on bouncing projects can give you weary eyes.

- The tighter your grip on your needle, the more you miss your mark. Ensure that you hold the needle lightly. When the wool starts to felt, and the surface gets bigger, you will begin to grip tighter to stab your needle inside the wool. Here, you should switch to a smaller needle.

- The working part of your needle is the fragile blade end. If it bends and flexes as you work, you should change your techniques to ensure that the needle moves in and out of your project work without much strain. If you face resistance as you work when the needle cannot pierce easily into your project, change into a smaller needle that goes in more comfortable, thereby saving your from tiredness, needle breakage, and injury.

- Working faster is not always better when it comes to needle felting. Going more quickly can be useful if you are only taking shallow jabs that pierce only the first 1/8 inches of your felting needle blade into your project. With deep thrusts, the faster you go, the more needles you will break, and the more mistakes you are bound to make.

- You can make your work as tight or dense as you want it. There are no hard and fast rules as to how firm or dense your work should be. However, the firmer your project is, the more likely it will break needles.

- Hold the needle so that you can view your fingers and stab slowly and carefully.

- Speed up your needle felting process with a needle felting pen.

- For round and uniform balls, stab your needle around your piece uniformly. Do not merely poke in the same direction, except you want to mold your wool to a particular shape.

- Do not force your felting needle to the wool. It can break. If your object becomes large and seems challenging to penetrate with your needle, then work at a slow pace so that you will not break your needle.

- Ensure that you use the right type of needle for the project you are on. Every stage of a project is different, and so is the needle you use for them. A lot of felters prefer to begin with a bigger needle before going for smaller needles.

- To avoid getting overwhelmed and burnt out, you need to start simple. However, simple does not necessarily mean boring. You can still create beautiful, simple designs through your creativity.

- Exercise patience, especially as a beginner. It can get frustrating, but please do not rush it. You will need ample patience to wade through the early stages and create beautiful pieces that will make you smile as you remember your progress.

- If your felting needle breaks and disappears in your piece, you can expose the broken needle by squeezing the piece gently. As you squeeze, do not put your fingers in the place that the end of the needle went in. You can gently pull out the needle with tweezers. Also, you can cut out the spot the needle disappeared with scissors and then find it. Immediately the needle is removed, felt the objects back with loose pieces of wood.

Tips on How to Finish Your Felted Works

- For facial details, do not use a lot of wool. You need tiny wool for eyes, mouths, and noses. It is easier to add more wool than to remove the whole piece and start all over.

- For the mouth and whiskers of your piece, you can use needle and embroidery thread to sew them on. This method is cleaner and more specific than felting a small strip of wool.

- If you want to make a child-friendly piece, it would be better to use wool for eyes rather than the black plastic eyes that come in kits that are bought separately. Also, never use melamine foam for your pieces; they can be dangerous when they are swallowed.

- When finishing your piece, tuck in the loose fibers by stabbing the surface gently. Then, trim loose fibers and smoothen the object.

- When you are attaching a small piece, you need to leave some loose fluff felt at the end of the smaller piece at the place you want it to connect to the more significant piece. Also, make an indent in the bigger piece in the particular spot that the smaller piece will enter with your needle, or cut out a small opening in the bigger piece with scissors and fill the tip of your smaller piece inside. Then, tighten the two pieces together with the needle.

- When your piece becomes firm and challenging to stab, it is almost ready.

- If you aren't cool with the finishing of your details, you can take off the top pieces with your needle. You can then add more felting wool to cover any gaps in your piece's body and remake the details.

- If your project has unwanted gaps or dents, take a tiny of the same colored wool, roll it into a small ball, and then felt it inside the opening using your needle. Continue to felt until it combines into the final piece and closes the gap.

- If you felt another piece of wool on a felted object, you should not felt the new wool down too hard because you may distort the shape of the felted object or lose the new felted wool inside the bigger one. You can stab the fibers of the wool into the main object with your needle so that it will remain in position.

Techniques for Needle Felting

Needle felting techniques can vary based on what you are making. After experimenting, you will know how to stab your felting needle into the wool to get different effects. However, the basics are as follows:

1. Prepare your wool. If you are using roving, tear out a piece of it out. You don't need to cut it; the roving will pull apart on its own easily.

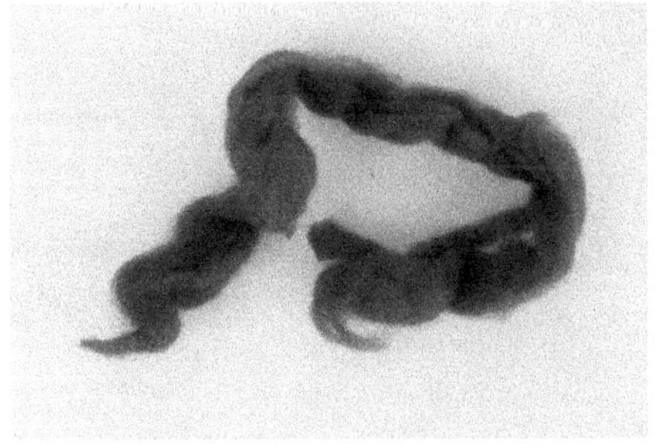

2. Roll your roving into a ball and make sure you tuck the ends in if you can.

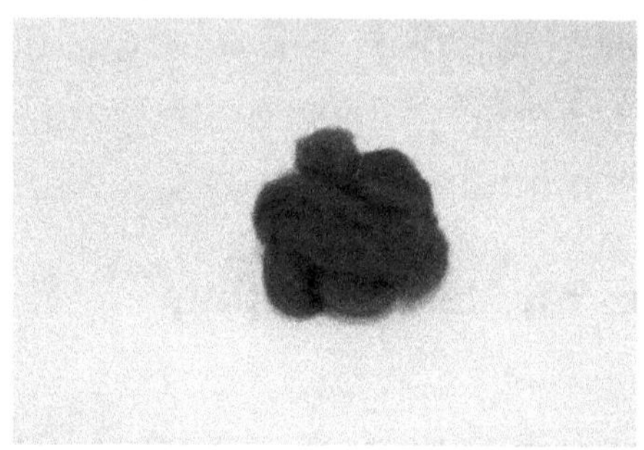

3. Poke the ball. Start by keeping the wool on top of your felting surface. Then start jabbing the ball with the needle, going in about ¼ inch deep every time. Poke straight up and down so that your needle will go in and out of the felt easy. Protect your fingers as you felt. Remember that felting needles are very sharp.

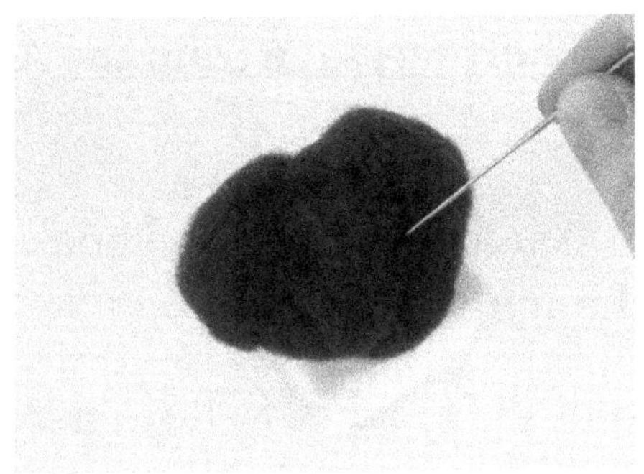

4. Continue until the wool felts. Keep stabbing the ball until the fibers begin to entangle together, and you will see the felt forming. By now, the ball has shrunk up a little. When stabbing the needle into a flat shape, the needle will sink into the foam mat, and the wool fibers get pushed through too. Therefore you have to keep lifting the piece of the carpet regularly not to get fastened onto it.

<u>A Short message from the Author:</u>

Hey, I hope you are enjoying the book? I would love to hear your thoughts!

Many readers do not know how hard reviews are to come by and how much they help an author.

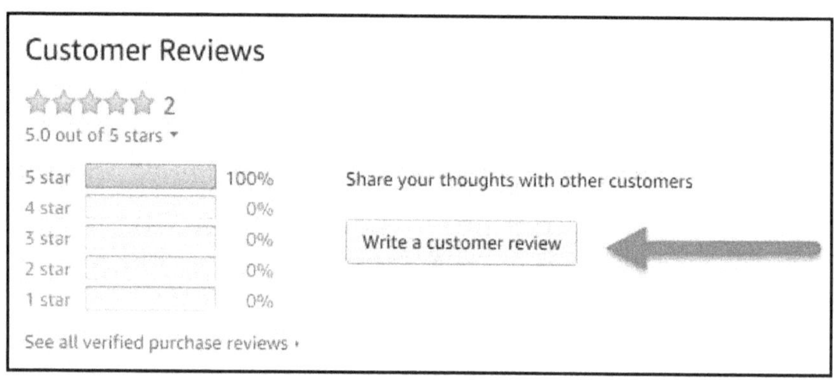

I would be incredibly grateful if you could take just 60 seconds to write a short review on Amazon, even if it is a few sentences!

>> Click here to leave a quick review

Thanks for the time taken to share your thoughts!

Chapter 4

Getting Started with Needle Felting

In the previous chapter, you have learned about the essential tips to note as you go about your needle felting projects. This chapter will focus on the basic tools and materials needed to get your needle felting projects off the ground and how you can get them to start creating awesome needle felted designs.

Essential Tools and Materials Needed

The necessary materials and tools that you require for needle felting are:

Felting Needle

These are a particular type of needle with rough tips. These tips help the fibers to be pulled to the middle of the wool to form a stiff felt. As you continue to poke with a needle, the fibers will become more rigid.

Felting needles are made from carbon steel, but they have various gauges, sizes, and blade styles. Depending on the combination of these factors, they can be described as "coarse," "medium," and "fine" needles. Coarse needles can be used for starting the work and felting a large amount of fiber together. On the other hand, more delicate needles are great for adding details and final smoothing of the wool surface. However, it is better to buy a variety pack that contains coarse, medium, and fine needles.

When you purchase your first felting needle, get one with a handle or get a handle separately. Even though you can do without a handle, it is a lot better and more convenient to have a simple wooden handle that will allow you to store the needle with the point protected.

If you want to felt fibers faster, you need to use a multi-needle tool. It makes any project go a lot faster.

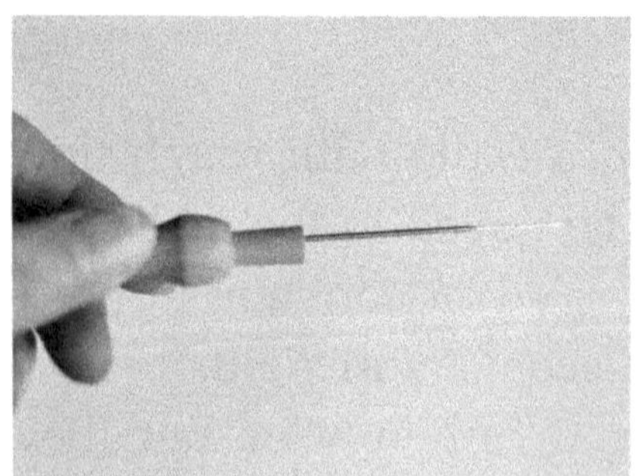 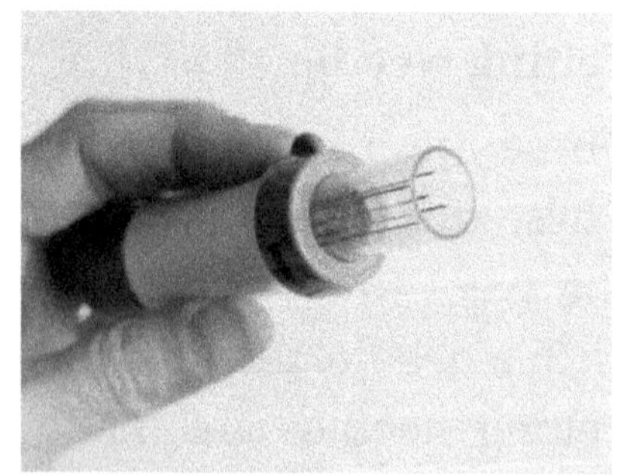

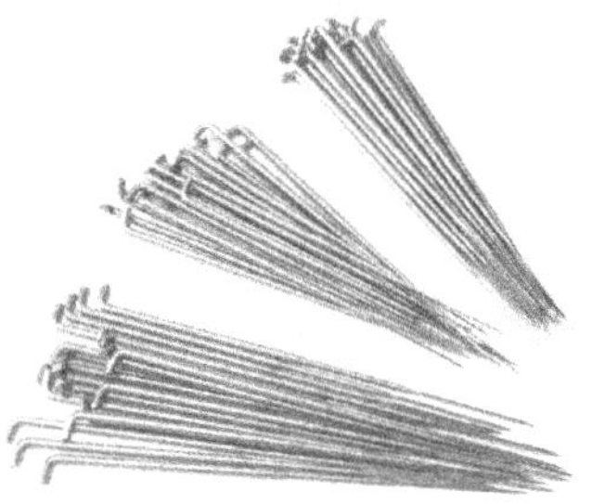

Needle Gauges: The different gauges for felting needles are 32, 36, 38, 40, and 42 gauges. As the gauges number increases, the needle becomes thinner. It would help if you used a thicker needle to felt coarse wool and smaller gauges for more delicate wool. When the wool becomes too thick, go for a smaller gauged needle.

If you have multiple needles, you might find it hard to identify the size of your needle. It is essential that you use nail polish or a small strip of colored tape at the handle.

Best Needle for Needle Felting
It would help if you had different kinds of needles in a collection of gauges. Some kits can also contain more than one needle. It would be best if you bought other

packets of needles at a lower price because you will break some needles as you proceed.

As a beginner, buying a 38-gauge needle is a good option. Also, a spiral or triangular needle will be best for a beginner. Reverse felting needles can serve as a finishing tool for manipulating the resulting texture or pulling out an underlying color if needed. However, it is not recommended if you want to go further with the craft.

Felting needles come with a different number of notches. A more significant number of grooves help for efficient felting, but it is unnecessary if you want to finish more detailed work. Always bear this in mind as you buy your needles.

Scissors

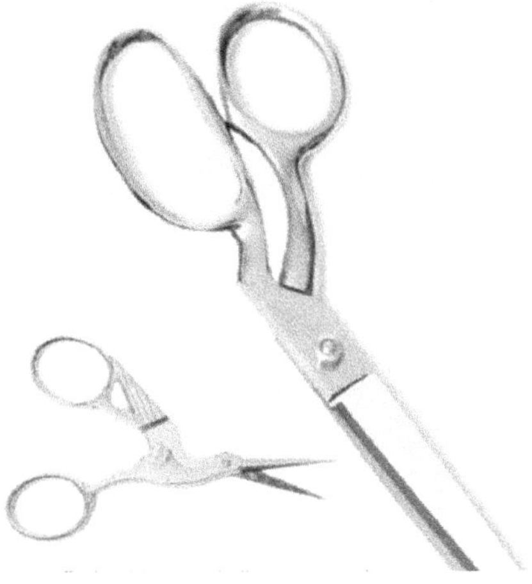

Here, embroidery and all-purpose with sharp blades are used which are necessary to get a clean edge when cutting the felt.

Needle Felting Wool

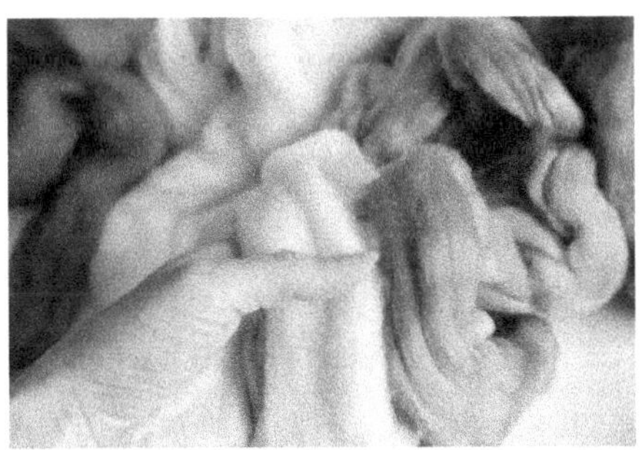

There are various types of fibers that you can select from for your project. You can use plant, animal, and synthetic fibers for this craft, but many felters prefer to use wool from sheep. Various sheep can produce wool with different characteristics, so you can work with varying types of wool to find your best. Examples are New Zealand, Merino, Drysdale, Norwegian Lincoln, Romney, and many others.

Wool is rated in microns, and the higher the micron, the more coarse the fibers. The fiber's roughness is not the only factor to consider in choosing your wool; you can also view the way the wool is processed.

Wool Batts and Wool Roving

Wool is available in two primary styles, which are batts and roving. Batts are thick wool that has not been wholly carded and therefore have fibers running in different directions. Roving is wool that has been brushed till the fibers are running in the same direction. Roving is best used for spinning.

Roving and batts are suitable for needle felting because you will use the needle to turn and manipulate the fiber kinks. Nevertheless, batts are more comfortable to use because the fibers run wild in various directions.

Carded Wool and Carded Slivers
Carded wool is also great for needle felting, and carded slivers (long lengths) are great for working around a wireframe where the finished project tends to be much softer. Carded wool sheets (batting) are also perfect for wrapping around a core base to make a lovely soft sculpture.

Best Wool for Needle Felting
Different wools work differently for needle felting. For instance, some wool is suitable for wet felting, such as Merino wool; however, they are not the best for needle felting.

Fine wool leads to the silkier, softer texture, while coarser wool is better for needle felting because the notches on the needle will grip on to the scales of the fiber easily. This will help you to handle the wool more efficiently.

Therefore, you need to go for medium-coarse fiber. It would be best if you went for wool that will be easy for the needle to grip but also with a smooth finish.

Examples of wool are:

- Merino wool (fine-medium): It is used for needle felting and wet felting.
- Icelandic wool (coarse, hairy): The undercoat (Thel) felts better than the outer coat (tog)
- Romney wool (medium-coarse): Can be very soft.
- New Zealand wool (medium-coarse): Suitable for needle felting and has a rougher finish than Merino.
- Shetland wool (medium-coarse): It can include coarse hairs that are hard to felt.
- Corriedale wool (medium-coarse): Suitable for both needle and wet felting.
- Norwegian wool (medium-coarse): It is better for needle felting, but is more coarse than Corriedale and Merino.

Below is a table that gives more information on the type of wool:

WOOL	ORIGIN	TEXTURE	MICRON	GOOD FOR NEEDLE FELTING
Shetland	Scotland	Medium/coarse	25-30	Yes
Swaledale	Northern	Very	36-40	Yes – Slightly wiry
Jacob	England	Coarse	25-35	Yes. Earthy finish
Corriedale (Merino and Lincoln cross)	New Zealand	Fine/Medium	25-30	OK – Requires more work, good for topcats, pictures, wet felting and blending.
Herdwick	North West England	Very Coarse	36 – 40	Yes – Very wiry finish
Merino	Spain	Fine	23	No – Best blended with coarser wool. Good for topcats, pictures, wet felting and blending.
		Super Fine	18	
White Faced Woodland	England	Coarse	28 – 38	Yes

Masham		Coarse	34 -38	Yes – Smooth finish Quite slippery
Blue Faced Leicester		Fine	24-28	Somewhat – Smooth finish. More visible needle marks.
Manx Loaghtan	Isle of Man	Medium/Coarse	27 -33	Yes
Border Licester	Northern England	Coarse	30 – 40	Yes – Smooth finish
Lincoln Longwool	England	Coarse	33-45	Yes
Teeswater	England	Coarse	30 -36	Yes – Smooth finish
Alpaca	South America	Fine	26	No
Gotland	Sweden	Medium/Coarse	27-35	Yes
Texel	Netherlands	Medium/Coarse	26 – 26	Yes
Norweigian	Norway	Coarse	28 -35	Yes

Needle Felting Foam

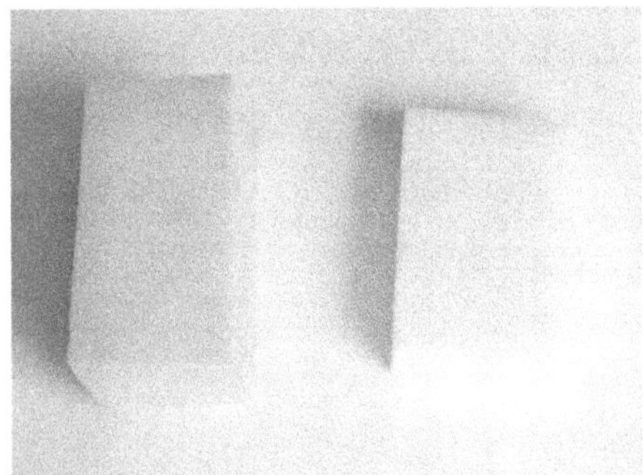

This is used for keeping your creation grounded as you work on it. It helps to protect your fingers and surfaces from needle damage. Some felter like using a coarse brush. However, a massive piece of foam works great. You don't need to buy one because you can get various alternatives that are around your house.

Felting Needle Pens

They are pens that can enhance your felting. The pen can hold a variety of needles at once (up to 3), thereby making felting faster and more efficient. It has a solid grip attached to it, and that makes it easier to handle. There are different types of tools that can help with common needle felting challenges. You can use other needle pens as you delve more into this art.

Bamboo Skewers

This is optional. However, it will greatly help you make small objects, long thin objects, and cone-shaped objects. You only need one, and you can also use them for non-felting art projects.

Dog Brushes

This is another item that you need for needle felting. Preferably, it would be best if you had the biggest that you can get. They are used to blend fiber either to make shades or to combine a transition better. They can also be used to clean your foam by scraping over the top of it with just the bottom part of the teeth. Dog brushes can be used to clean hand carders, a blending board, or even a drum carder.

Lint Rollers

They are used in cleaning your felting mat after you either rub most of the fiber off with your hand and gently scrape it with the dog brush. After using the dog brush to clean your mat, the lint roller also helps to pick up any foam bits that you were not able to shake off, so they do not end up in your work.

Chapter 5

Crafting Needle Felting Projects

Now, we have come to the cruise of this book. This chapter will guide you through many needle felting projects to give you a head start on your needle felting craft, starting from the easiest to the more advanced projects. Also, the projects include both animate and inanimate objects. The best way to learn these projects is to practice them. I have also added clear pictures to guide you on the steps.

So, let's start crafting!

DIY Elbow Patch

This is a great project for beginners. It can help to beautify your clothes and make them stand out.

Things You Need:
- Wool sweater
- Piece of dense foam or needle mat
- Wool roving
- A 36 gauge felting needle

- A 3" heart cookie cutter
- An iron

Directions

1. Put on the sweater, and put a piece of tape about one half of an inch underneath the elbow. Carry out the same with the opposite elbow. Put off the sweater and add the foam block to one of the sleeves.

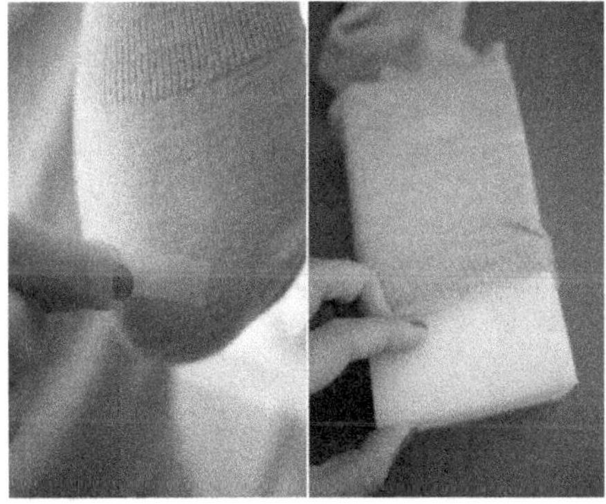

2. Line up and center the bottom of the cookie-cutter across the top of the tape. Take little tufts of wool.

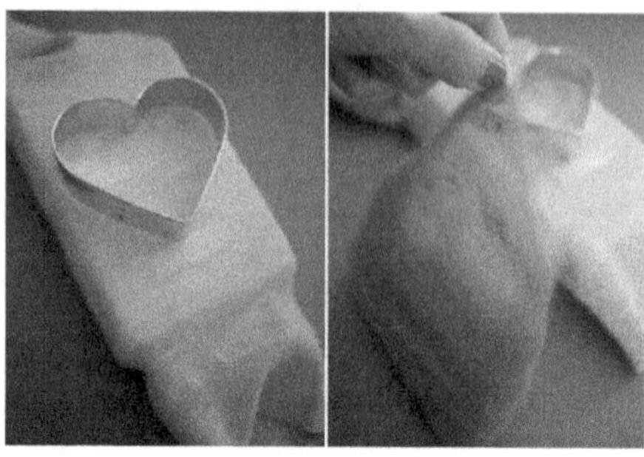

3. Fill up the cutter, by spreading the wool fibers uniformly.

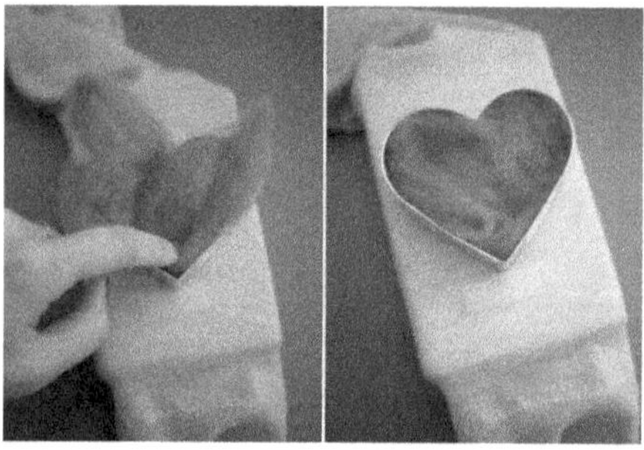

4. Felting needles have small, sharp burrs that grab and entangle the wool fibers. As you hold the needle vertically, continue to stab it on the wool roving through the sweater. It is simpler to work around the outside perimeter of the cutter before proceeding inside.

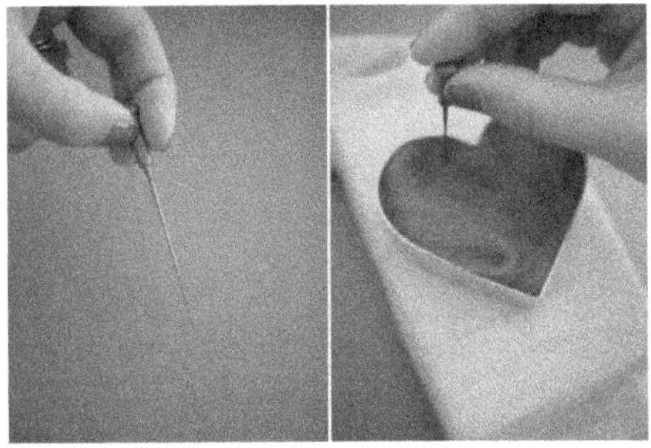

5. Continue to stab till the surface becomes flat and uniform.

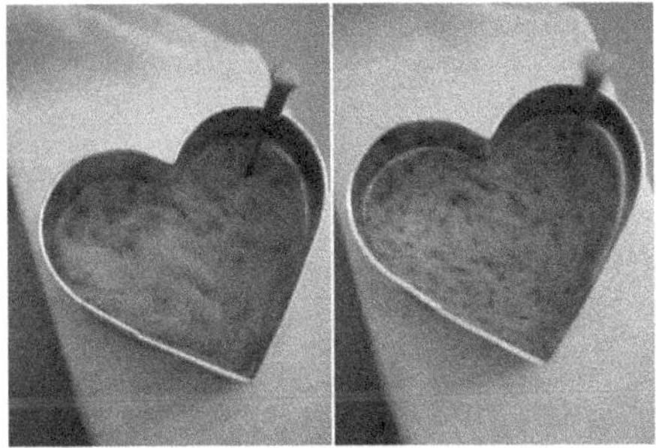

6. Take off the cutter and use the needle tip to take in any stray fibers. Do not be worried about the holes, because they will be filled later.

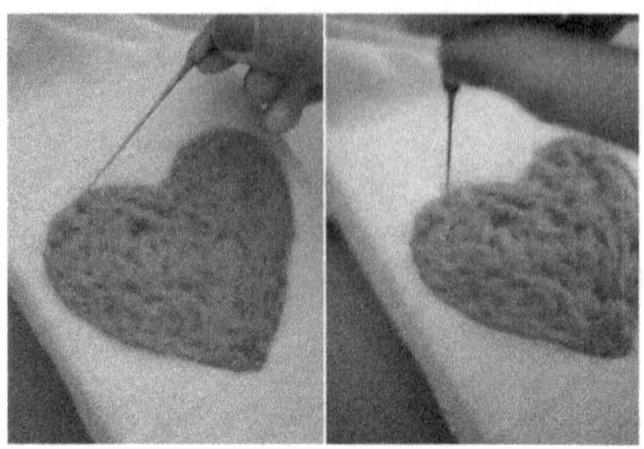

7. Cover up the uncovered or uneven spots by using more wool roving where required.

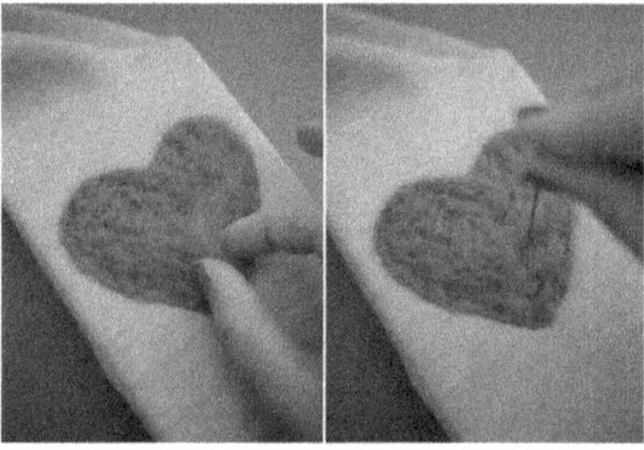

8. Free the sweater from the foam carefully. You will discover that the fibers have moved through to the back of the sweater.

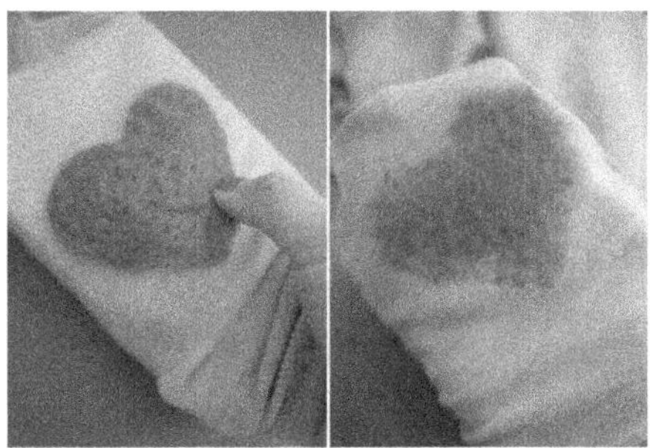

9. You can smoothen the patch by sprinkling with water and then press with an iron on the wool setting.

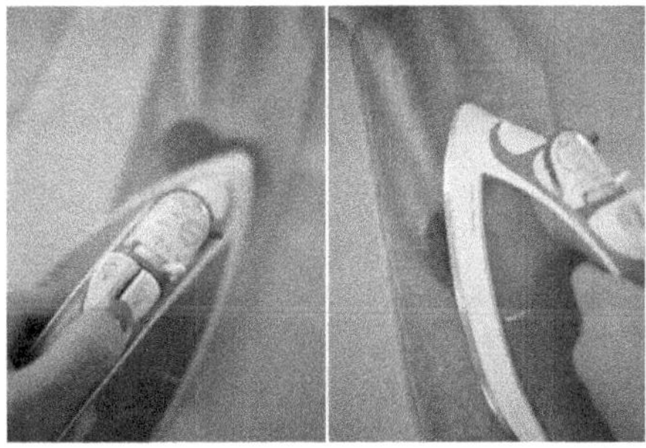

10. Repeat the same steps on the second sleeve. Your elbow patches are completed.

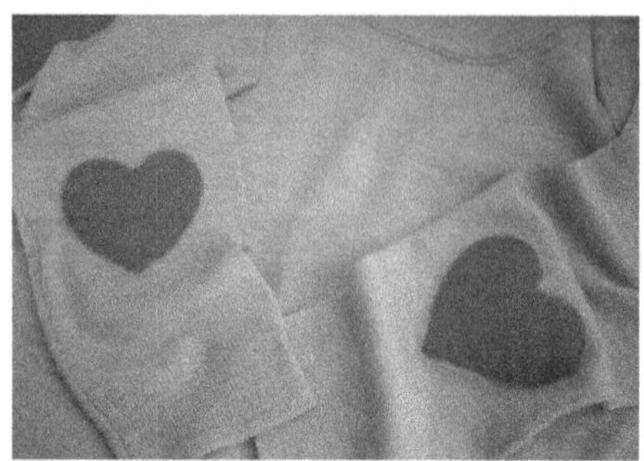

Felted Rainbow Pillow

This is another simple project that will not take a lot of your time. It is also ideal for beginners. If you want to make pillows to decorate and add color to your home, this is the craft for you.

Things You Need:

- ½ Yard of medium weight white fabric.
- Fabric scissors
- Pencil
- Needle felting tool
- Roving wool
- Needle felting mat
- Pins
- Thread

- Hand sewing needle
- Sewing machine (recommended)

Direction

1. Fold fabric into two and cut out a pillow in the circle size you want across the fold. You can use a big circular object like a bowl as a pattern to have a full circle of fabric that can fold to a rainbow shape.

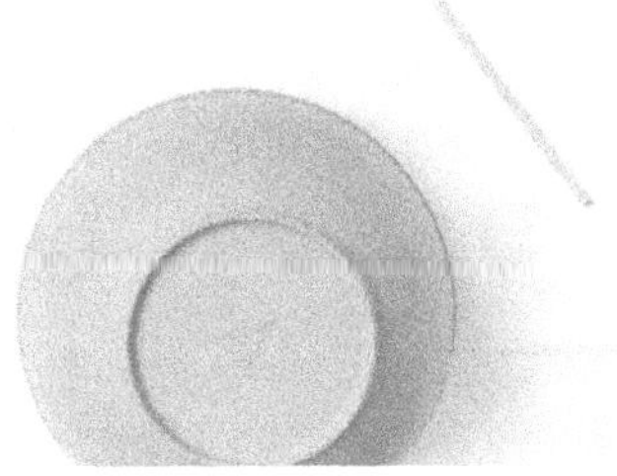

2. With a pencil and ruler, mark where you want the lines of the rainbow to be. For this craft, the 8-inch circle had about 1-inch for each color, with a white space in the inside curve and across the outside for sewing.

3. Begin from one color, from the outside, take out a long piece of wool and place where the fold will be.

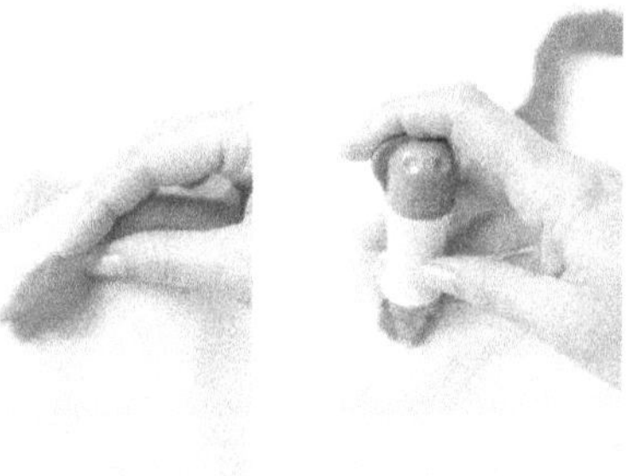

4. Keep the section of fabric on the needle felting mat and place the wool where you desire it. Begin to stab to set in the wool into the fabric.

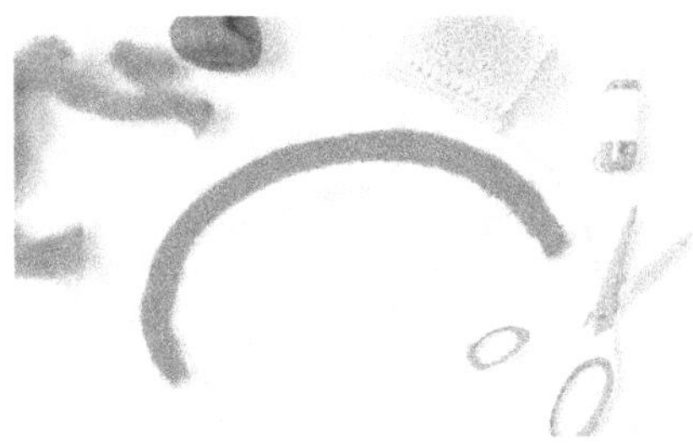

5. Change the fabric's position as required so that it will stay over the needle felting mat as an arc around the outside of the fabric. You can add more wool and continue if you run short of wool.

When you get to another side of the rainbow, cut away the excess before needle felting the area.

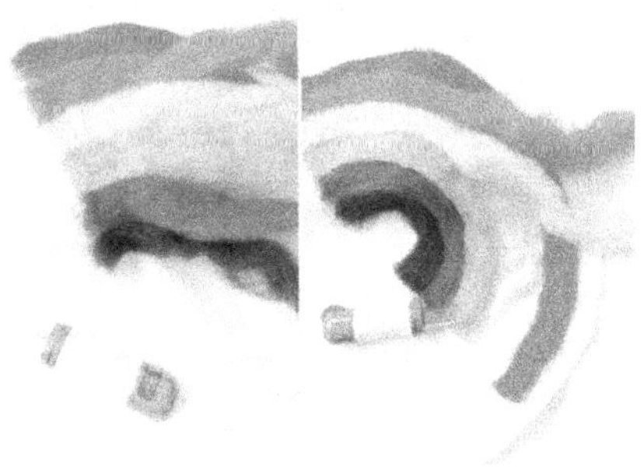

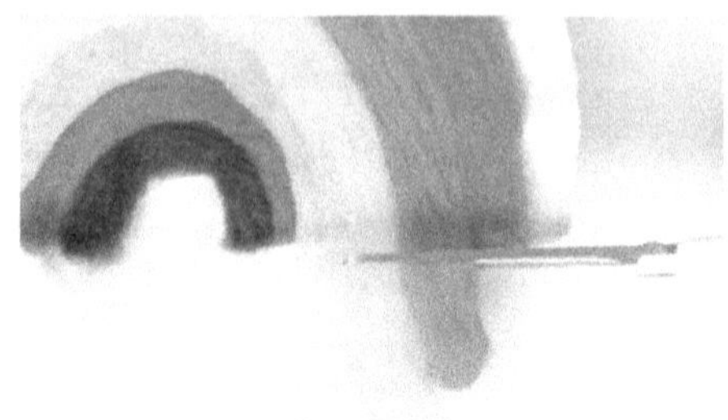

6. Let the colors be next to one another. You can work on one color per time or work on multiple colors as you move along the fabric. It is your shot to call.

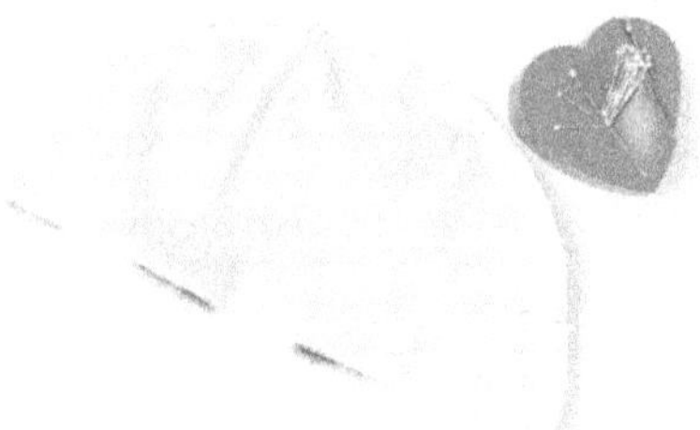

7. After finishing the needle felting, fold the fabric to a semi-circle shape so the felted pattern is inside, pin round the ends, and leave one section open.

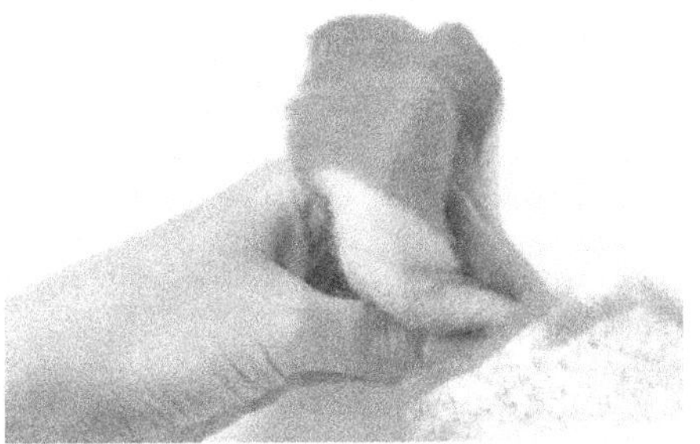

8. Sew about the semi-circle, and leave one section open. Cut loose threads, and draw the pillow right side out via the opening.

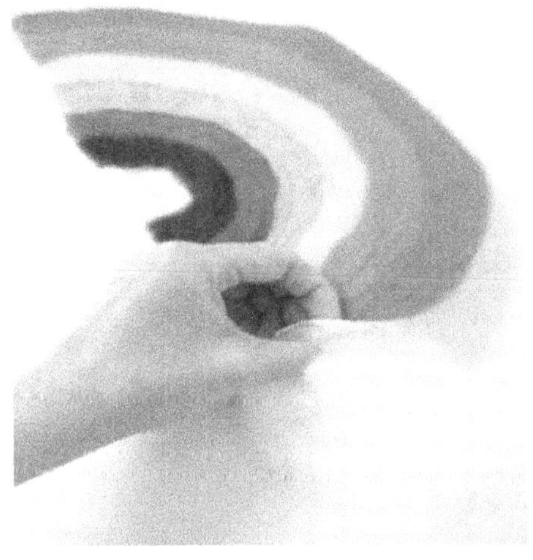

9. Fill the pillow to your desired firmness

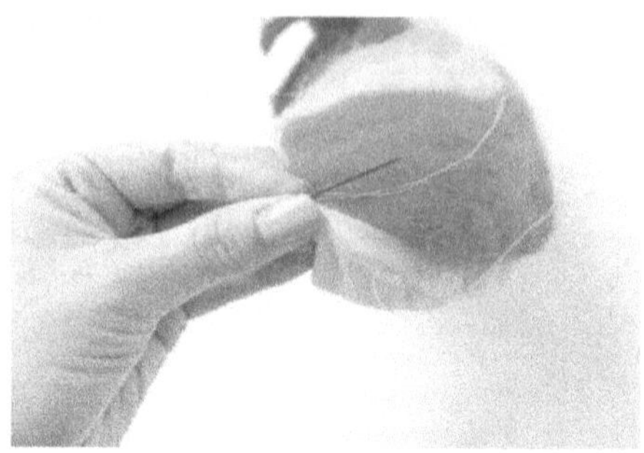

10. Sew through the opening with a hand sewing needle and thread to make an invisible stitch to finish the pillow.

You can place your new felted rainbow pillow on a bed or chair with other pillows to add more color to your room.

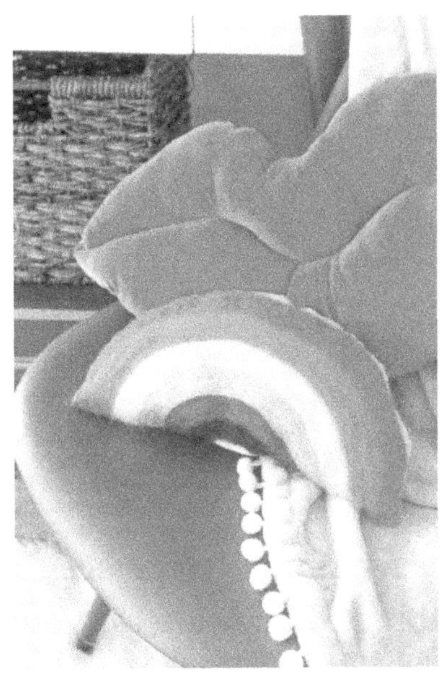

Rustic Robin Needle Felting (3D Needle Felting)

For this project, you need to felt the different parts and then join them together.

Directions

Body

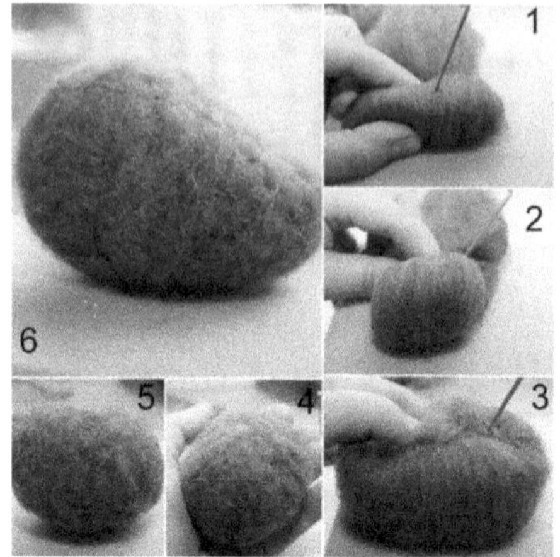

1. Divide the wool into two pieces, pull them apart gently and keep half aside for your other Robin.

2. Begin with a long strip of wool and roll it to a coarse ball shape, and tuck in the split edges as you continue. Begin with less wool than you need and add as you continue.

3. Pierce the wool as you go round, thereby tangling and locking the fibers together, holding the needle straight till the fibers begin to entangle together and hold its shape. You should continue turning while felting so that you will not make dents in a part of the body.

4. Keep felting till you get your desired size and shape, and compare with the size template.

5. After achieving a rough egg shape, with the narrower end as the Robin's rear, roll it gently between your hands. It helps to smoothen and shape the body and hide serious needle marks.

6. Press and felt the narrower end to flatten a bit. Your tail gets attached here. The finished body shape will be soft but gets back to shape as you press it.

Body Color

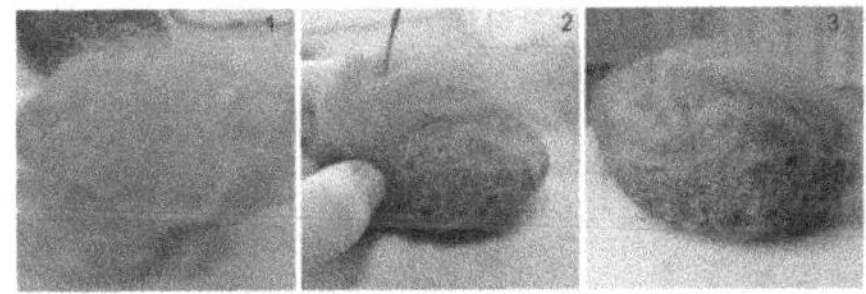

1. Combine orange and a little red wool roving with your hands. You can add more red based on the color you prefer.

2. Gently attach to the base of the body, bringing the color almost halfway up.

3. Keep felting till your color is loosely attached. This combination adds contrast and makes it look more natural.

How to Make the Tail

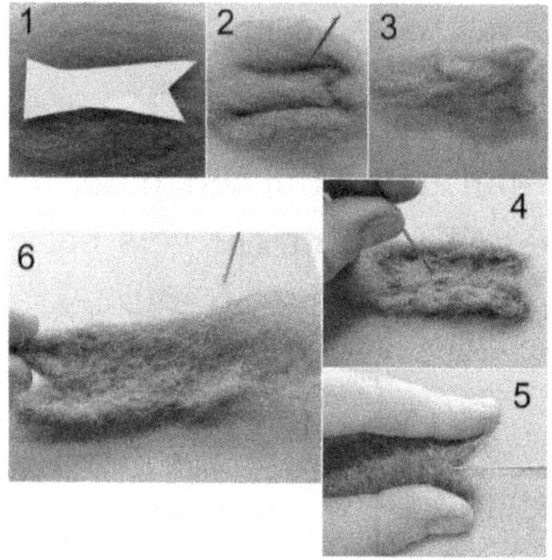

1. Cut out a tail pattern and keep on a fine layer of wool on your foam block. You can draw a rough shape around the pattern.

2. Remove the pattern and check the lines you drew.

3. Fold the edges and gently felt, based on the line of the shape you created, and leave the end free so you can easily felt it to the body.

4. Continue to turn and felt until it is firm.

5. Grip the tail's sides and create a fork's shape by gently poking the needle repeatedly via the center, and be careful not to stab your fingers.

Remember to always keep your needle straight to avoid breaking the tips.

How to Attach the Tail

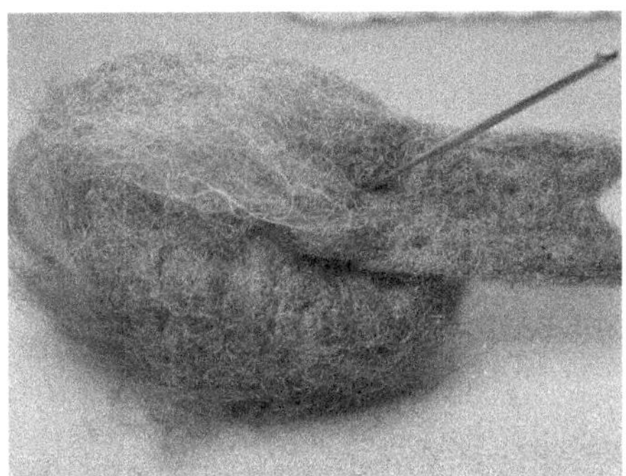

1. You attach the tail by felting the tail's loose end to the narrower end of the body. If the tail is secured, you don't need to bother about any loose wool because you can felt over it, but you need to keep it loose to give a more natural look.

How to Build the Head

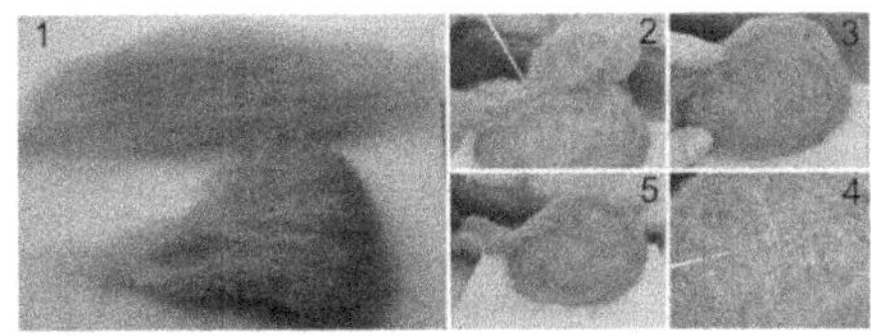

1. Pull wool of length of approximately 10cm from the remaining wool. Ensure that you have

leftover wool for the beak and wings. Fold the wool in half and twist the end gently to form a rough petal shape.

2. Gently fix the narrow end to the top half of the body, which is the wider end, and then felt into place.

3. Continue to hold on to where you just felted and keep felting the remaining loose wool; it will give more dimensions to your craft.

4. Felt at the sideways to minimize needle marks and retain the shape.

5. This is the finished body.

How to Make the Wings of the Robin

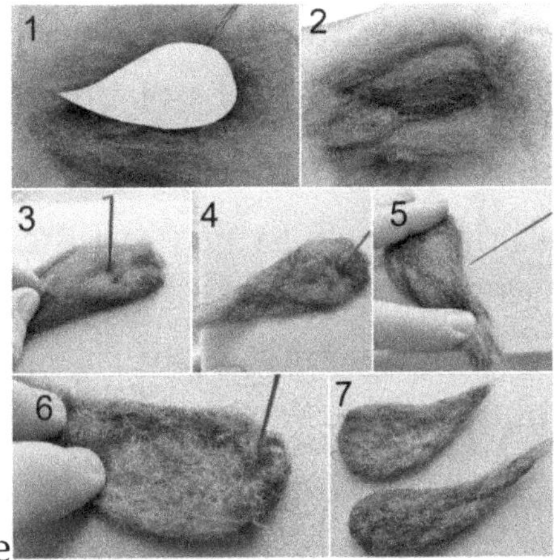

1. Blend a small layer of dark brown, brown and a little orange wool and keep on your foam block. Cut a wing pattern and lay on the layer of wool. Draw a rough shape with your needle like you did when you were creating the tail.

2. Take out the wing pattern and check the lines you drew again.

3. Fold the sides and gently felt, based on the line of the shape you created.

4. Continue turning and felting till it becomes firm and retain its shape. Ensure that it is firm.

5. Fold the corners of the wing and make a curve by gently poking the needle continuously across the top center, and you need to be careful not to prick

your fingers. Remember to hold your needles straight so that you will not break the tip of the needle.

6. Pull the edges over to tidy up the wing and felt more. Continue turning till you become satisfied with the whole shape. Continue the process for your other wing.

7. Determine the look you want your finished wing to have; you can bend the end over for a neat finish.

Completed Body Parts.

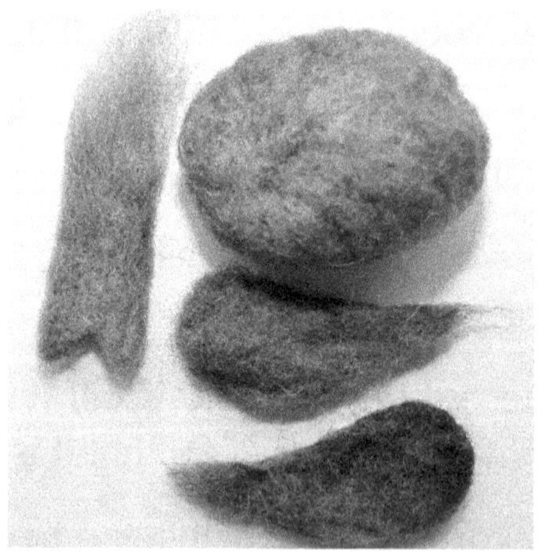

How to Attach the Wing of the Robin

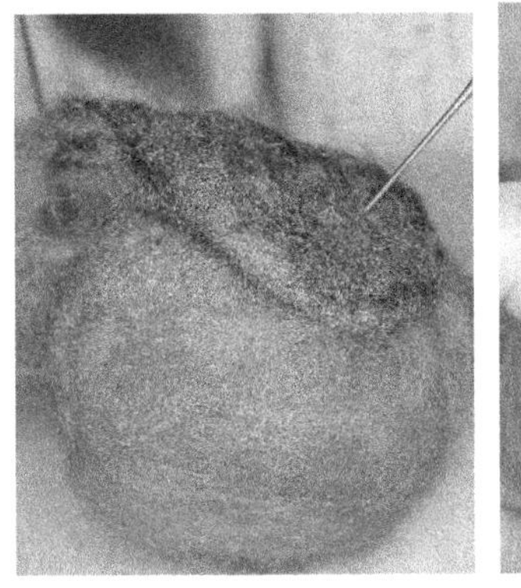 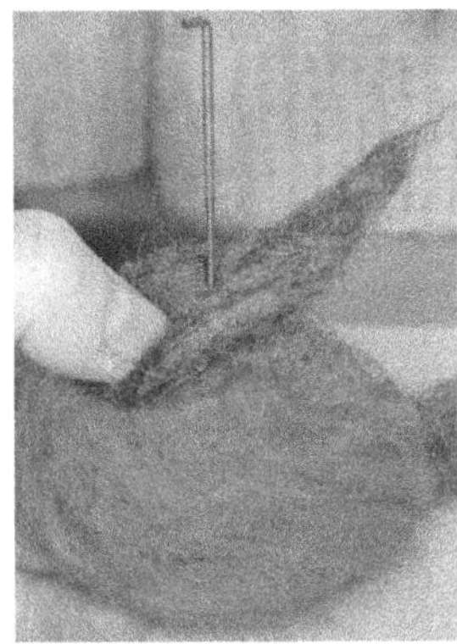

1. Felt the wing to the side of the body by stabbing the needle via different wing sides.

2. Replicate for the other side. Note that wings can either be up or down based on your personal preference.

How to Make the Beak

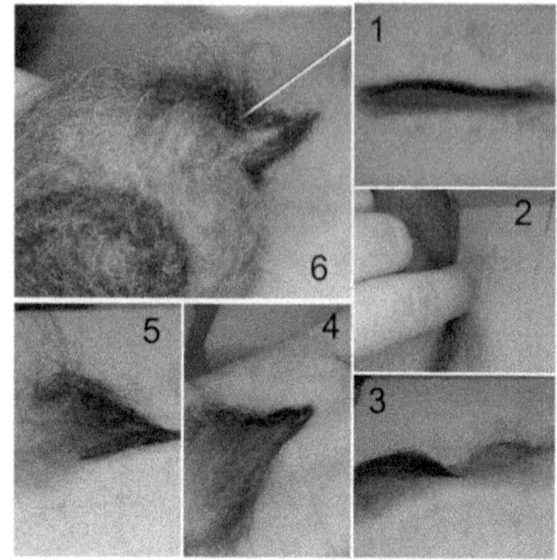

1. Combine together the fine length of dark and light brown.
2. Hold in the center.
3. Squeeze together while rolling it between your fingers.
4. Fold the wool into half and roll the end in the palm of your hand to produce the point of the beak.
5. Leave an end loose so you can attach it to the face. Gently felt so you don't distort the face.
6. You are almost there. There are just little finishing touches to add

How to Make the Eyes

1. For the left eye, take the black thread and needle from your sewing kit and sew from a side of the face to another for several times so it can be secured.

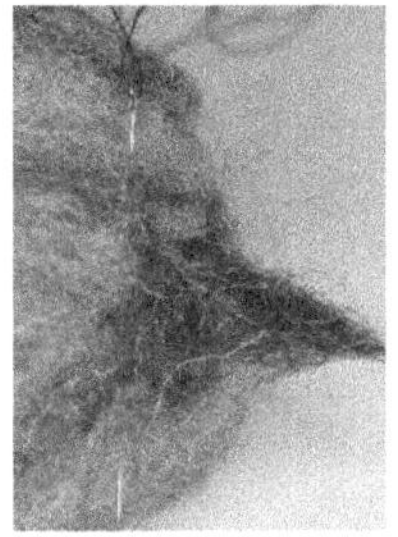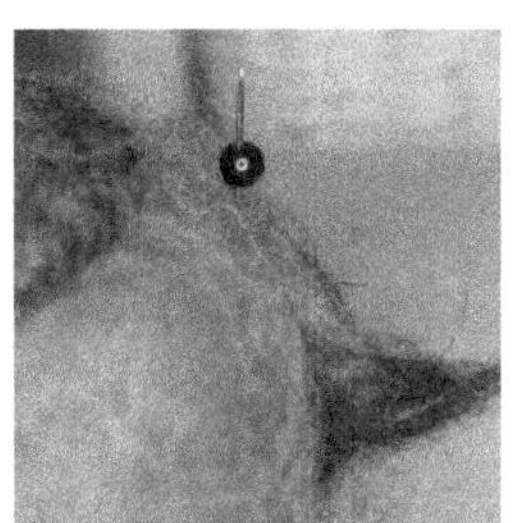

2. As soon as the thread is secure, place the bead on the end of the needle and sew through for more times to keep the bead in position.

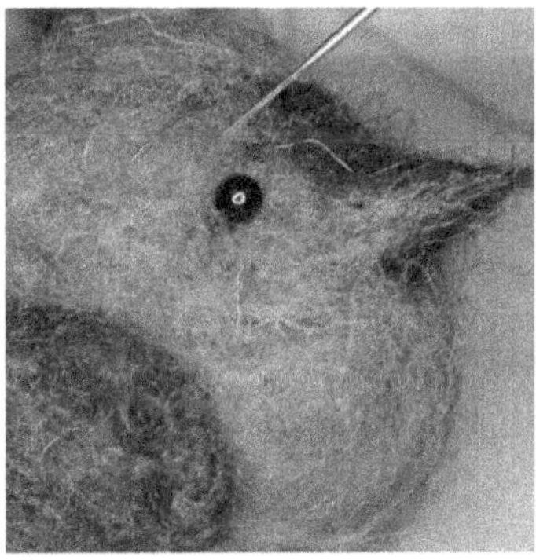

3. You can now sew to the other side and place your second bead on the end of the needle to put in the other eye.

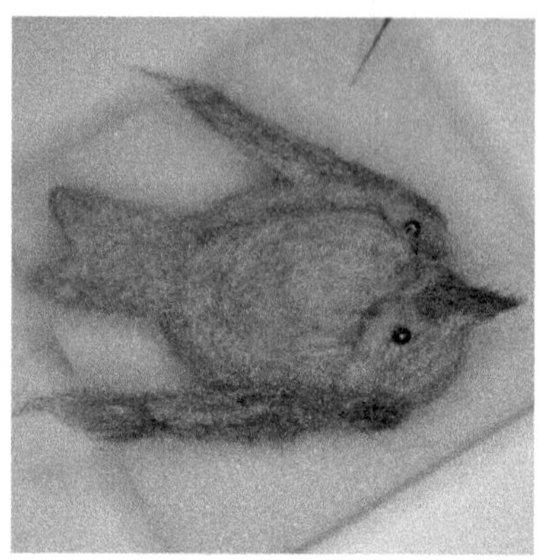

4. Complete your Rustic Robin by placing some highlights above the eyes and the body also.

Needle Felted Dog

Things You Need:

- Coarse wool (black and ochre color)
- Small black merino wool for facial features
- Foam pad
- Small scissors
- Thin felting needle and reverse felting needle
- 2 round black 3 mm beads.
- Black cotton and needle.

How to Create the Body

1. Fold 10g of ochre wool to a tight sausage shape, and leave them thicker at one side. Work on the pad, continue to hold the thicker end, and uniformly stab the thinner end with the fine felting needle until the wool becomes smooth, firm and rounded.

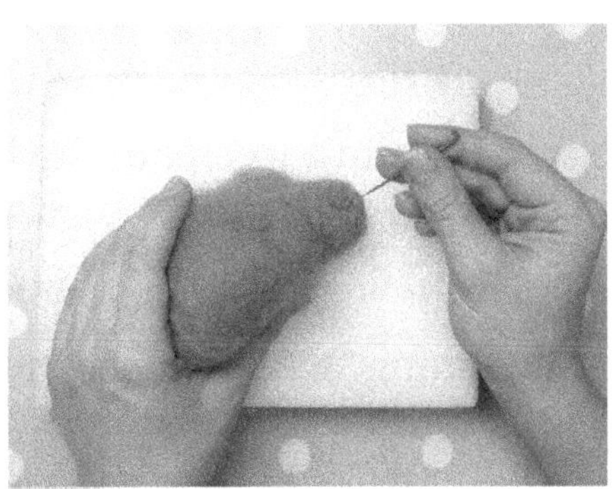

As you work down the body, stab the thicker end till it becomes rounded and firm. Put the body on the pattern to check whether the shape is accurate.

How to Make the Back Legs

1. Fold a sausage of wool thicker at one corner. Keep the wool on the pad and start felting the thinner foot end to a sausage shape

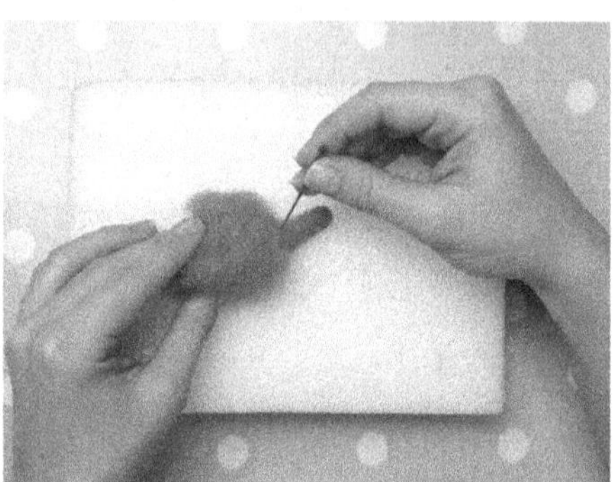

2. Fold the wool around to create the heel when the foot becomes firm. Continue to felt the remaining wool to finish the leg shape, allowing a few loose fibers for attaching. Create a second leg with the same method.

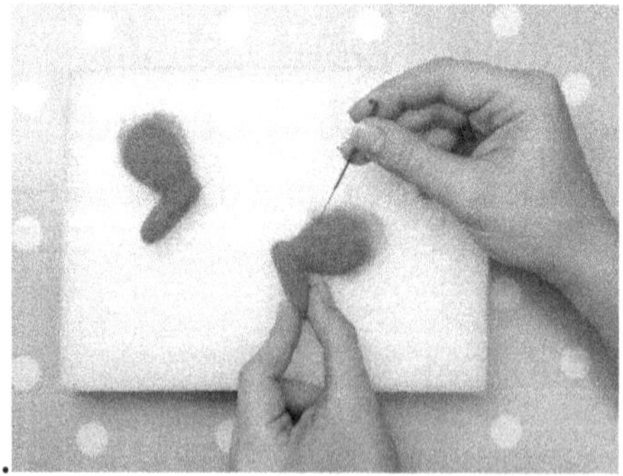

3. Spread out the loose fibers and push the leg on
    the thinner end of the body, felting the loose end
    in to secure.

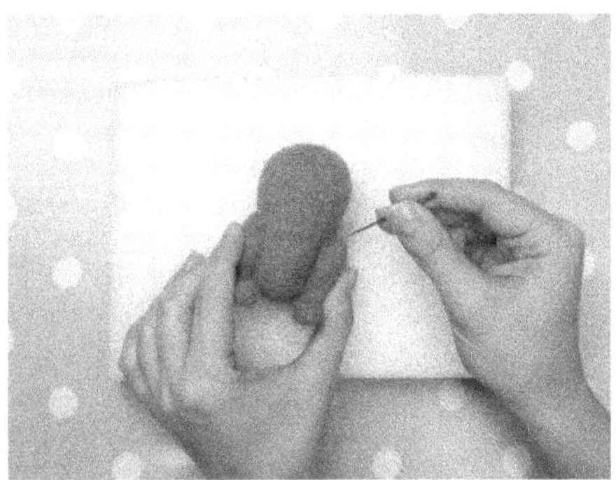

4. Fold a sausage of wool for the front limb. Felt a
    wounded end for the paw and allow loose fibers
    at the other side.

    Create another one with the same method.

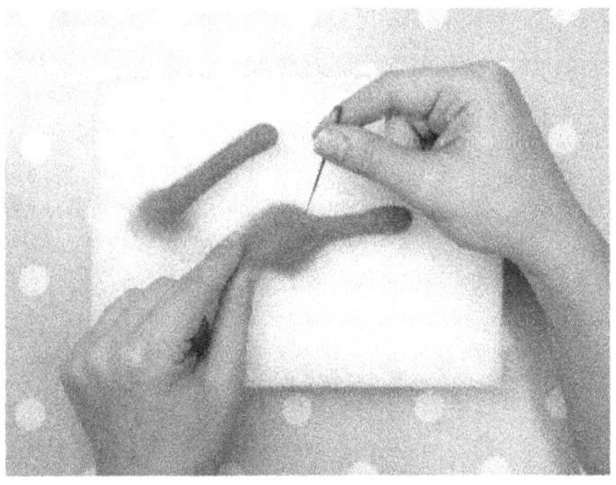

5. Push the front leg on the body so the paws will be angled slightly outwards and aligned with the body base. Felt the loose fibers into the body to secure it.

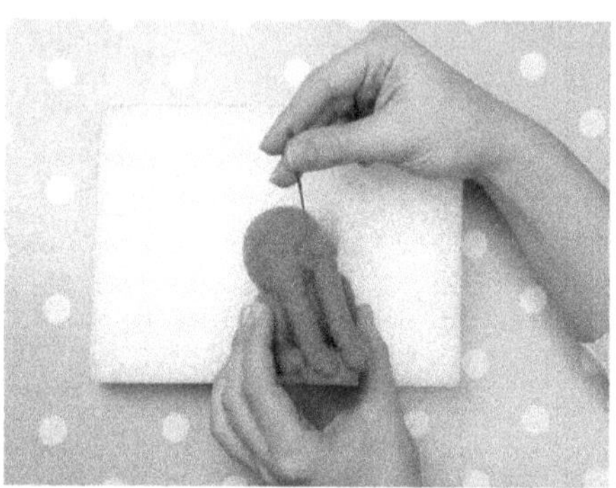

How to Felt the Head

1. Based on the template, felt the head and muzzle shapes, and leave the loose fibers as shown.

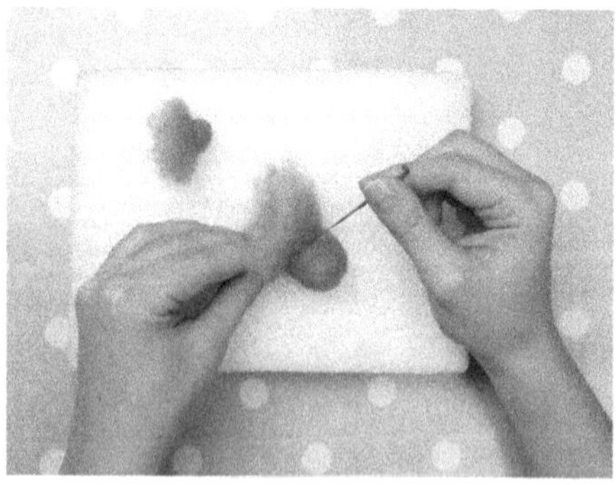

2. Keep the muzzle on the head and felt the loose
   fibers to fix the muzzle.

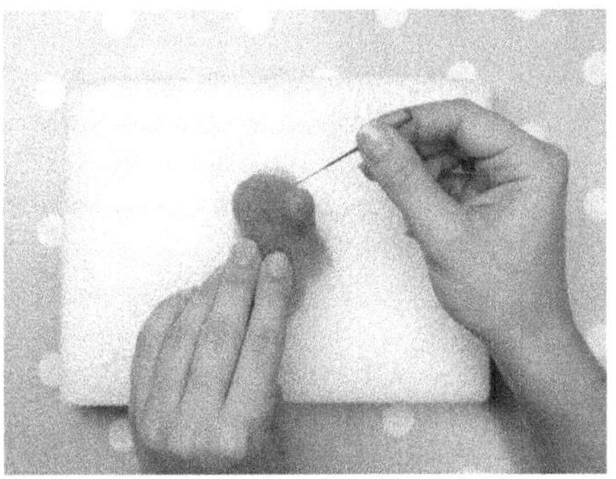

3. Felt the head on the body.

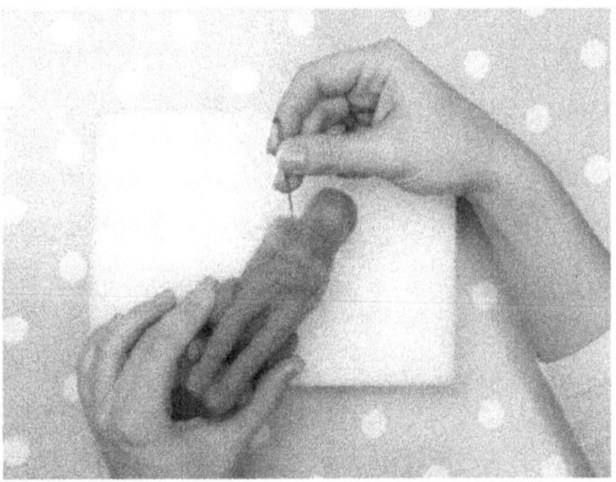

4. Felt with little black merino wool to serve as eye
   patches.

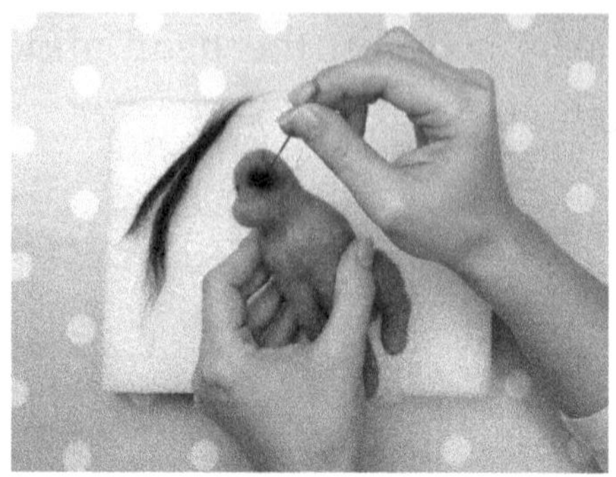

5. Felt the nose with thin length of merino wool, needling at the sides to form a triangle. Then fill in.

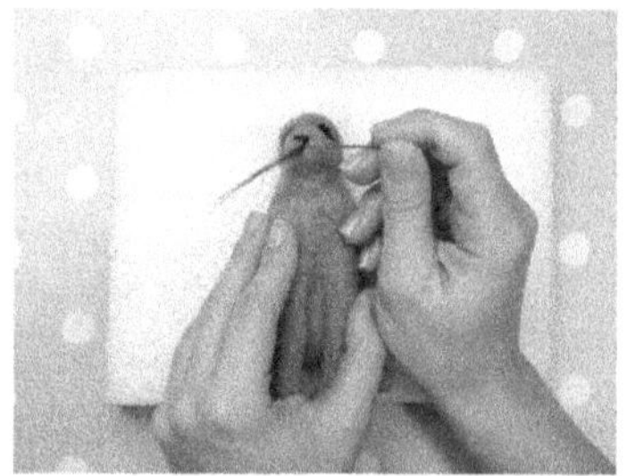

6. Felt the mouth carefully, beginning with a length that comes down from the nose, and then work outwards.

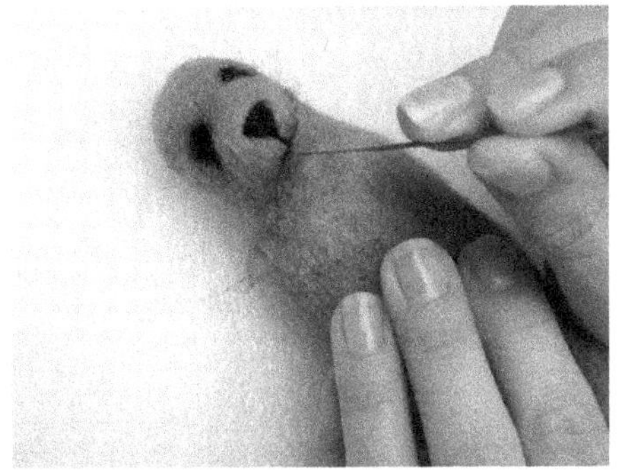

7. Sew on the eyes by threading a needle and cotton from the back of the head via an eye batch. After that, thread on a bead. Push the needle back through the head to secure the bead in place.

   Repeat for the second eye.

8. Tie both threads at the back of the head, then string them back via the head and cut the ends.

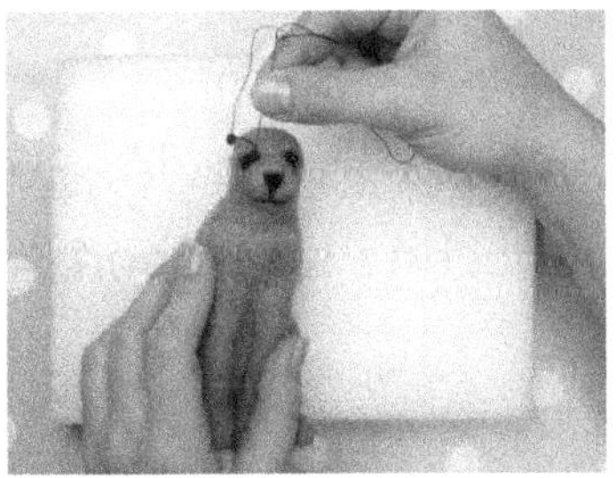

9. Felt the two black ears and leave little loose fibers at the root of each ear. Keep the ears in position and felt the loose fibers to secure it to the head.

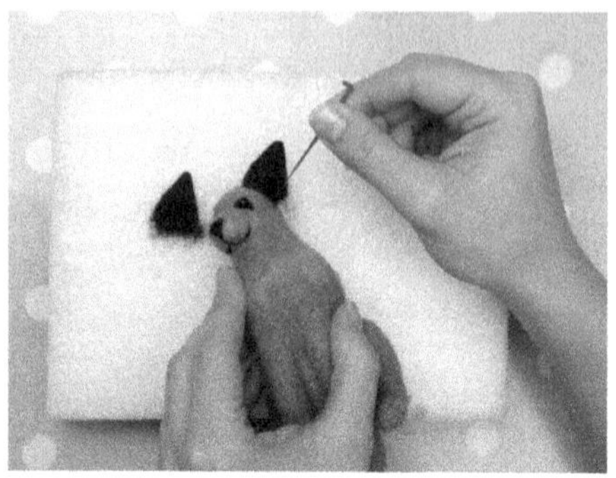

10. Fold the ears, and secure to the body by felting below the fold.

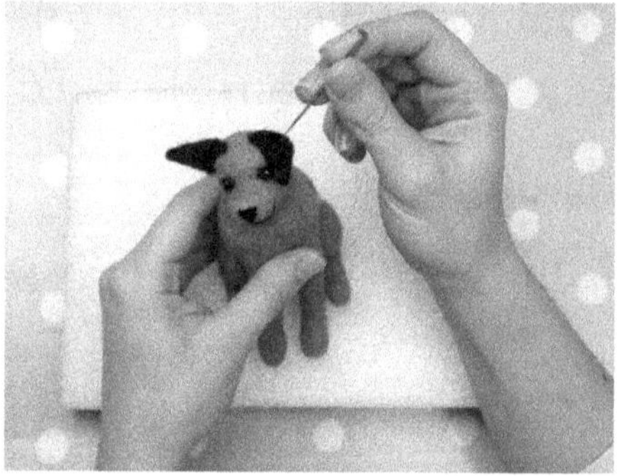

11. Felt the black tail by leaving loose fibers at the base and connecting to the body.

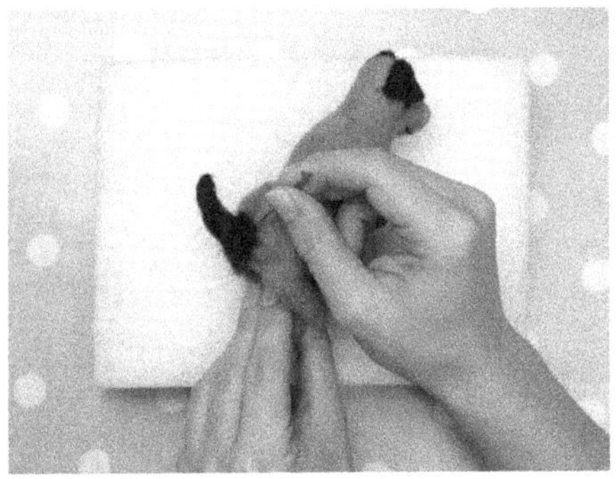

12. Place patches of black wool on the body and felt them flat and smooth.

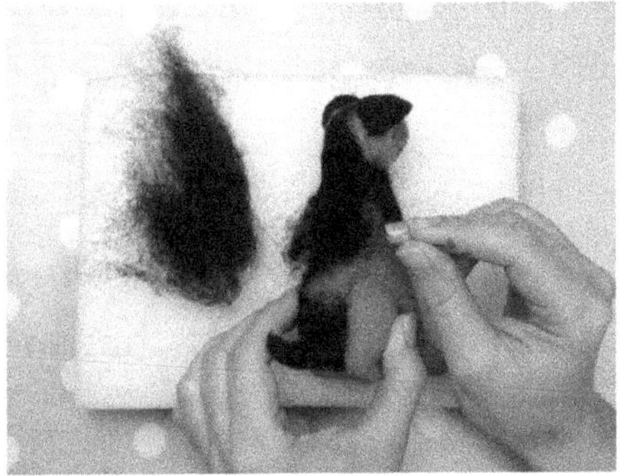

13. With a reverse felting needle, drag ochre fibers via the black patches to form the fluffy look.

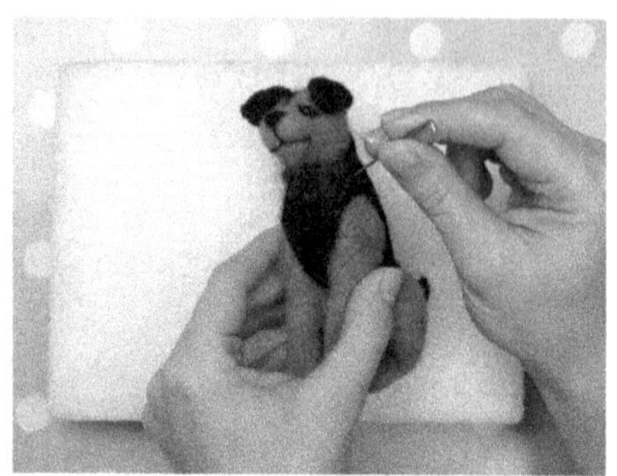

Felted Cat

This is a 3 dimensional project and will take some time for a beginner to craft. However, with enough practice, you will be able to pull it off.

Things You Need:

- Felting wool (2 colors, 1 for the cat and the other for the stripes)

- Felting needle

- Black felting wool (for the eyes)

- Sponge block

Directions

Make the Head

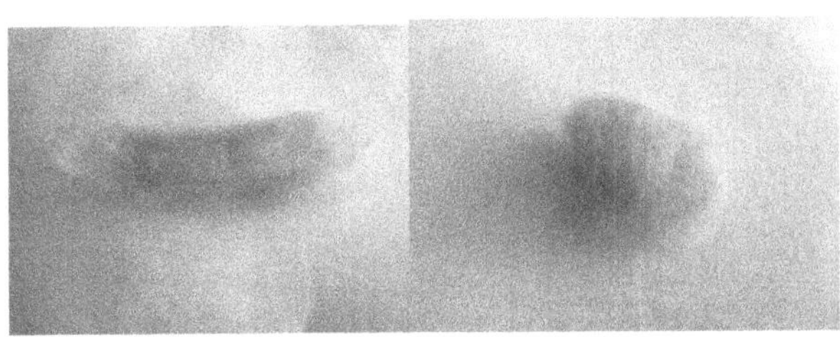

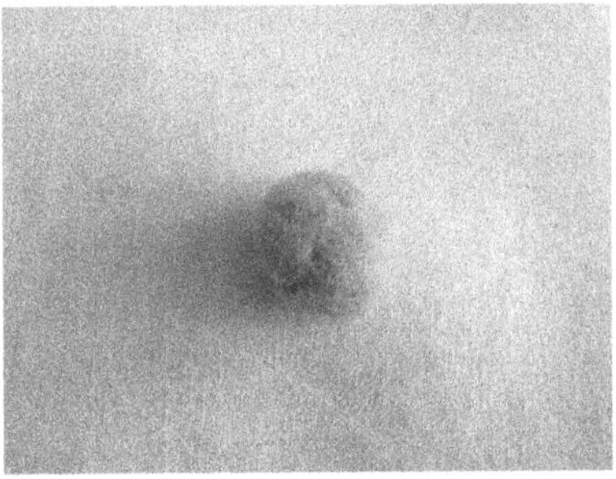

1. Roll the wool you want to use as the main color loosely with your finger. Do not roll it tightly; allow some space between your fingers. Now, stab your needle on the wool till it becomes a firmly packed ball.

Make the Body

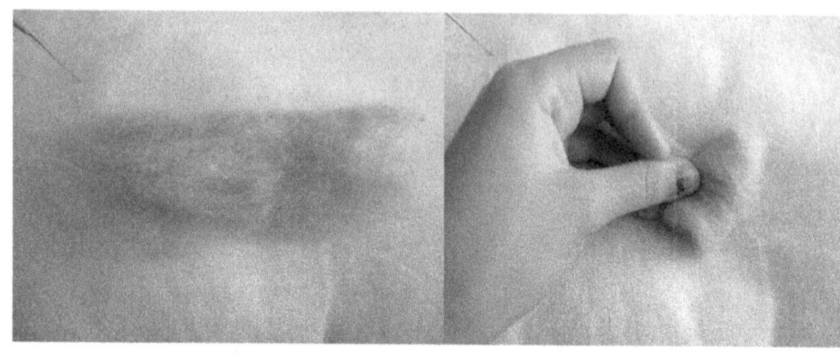

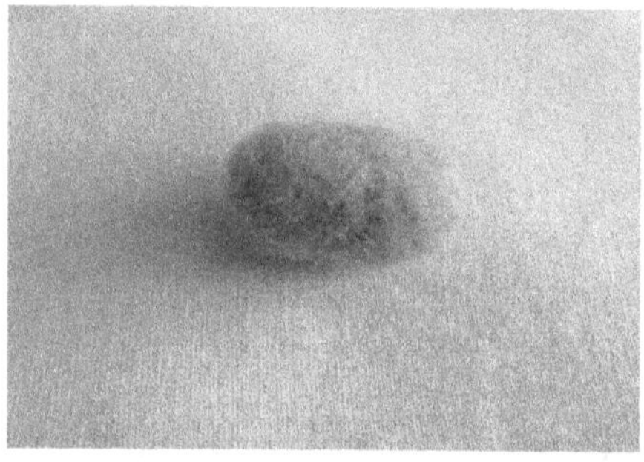

1. Take a big part of felting color, of the same color with the head, and then with your finger pads, form it to an oval shape loosely.

Attach the Body and the Head

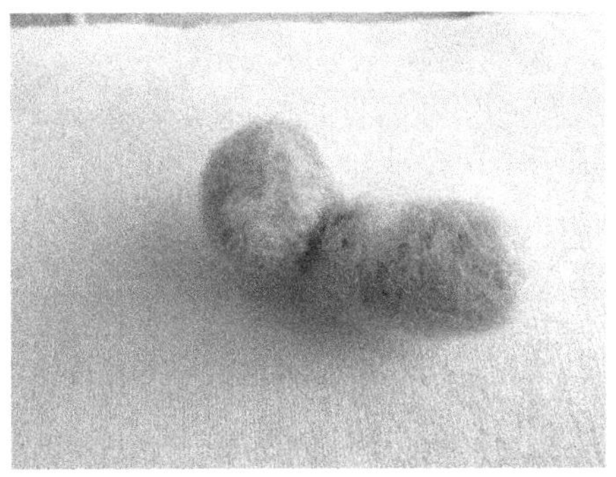

1. Now, get the head and set it at the position you desire it on the body. Stab with the needle within the neck part. Ensure that it is tightly connected.

Make the Paws

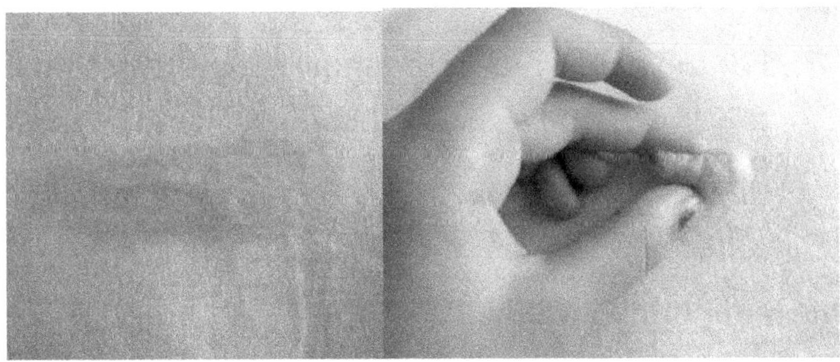

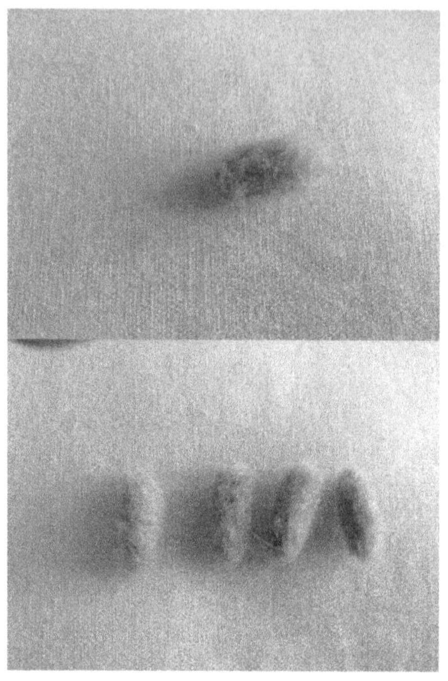

1. For the paws, repeat the same process you did for the body, only make them smaller and create four.

Attach the Body and the Paw

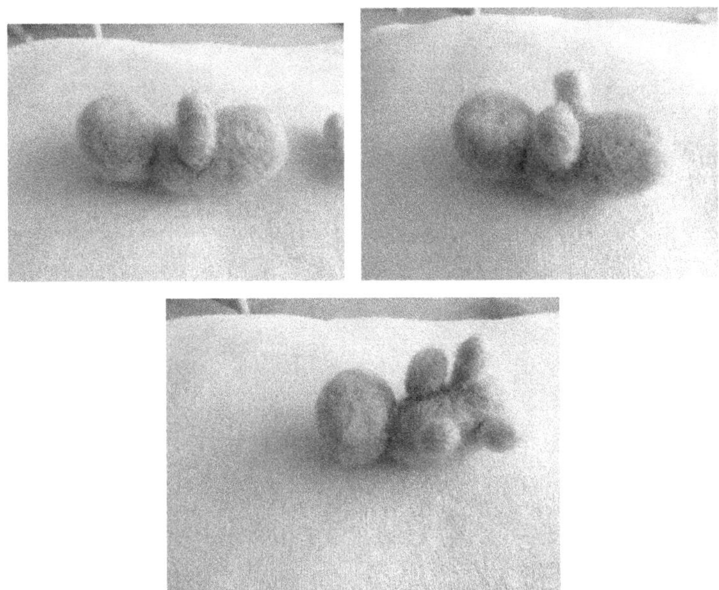

1. Get each of the paws and repeat the same process you carried out with the head. Stab with the needle at about 45-degree angle till they stay attached.

Make the Tail and Attach to the Body

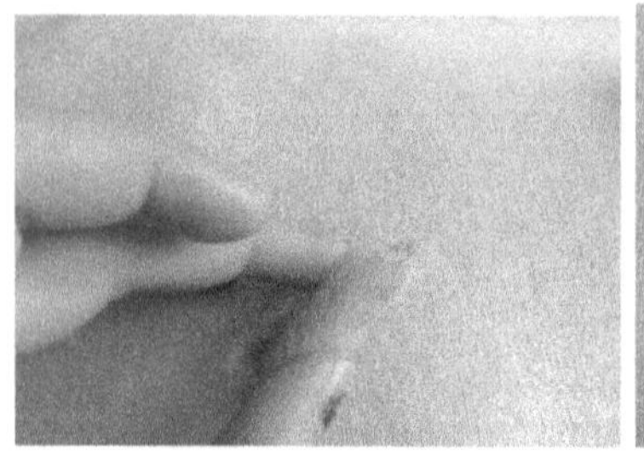 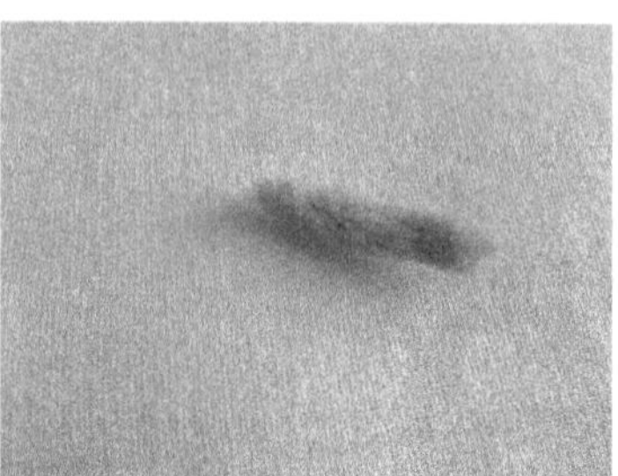

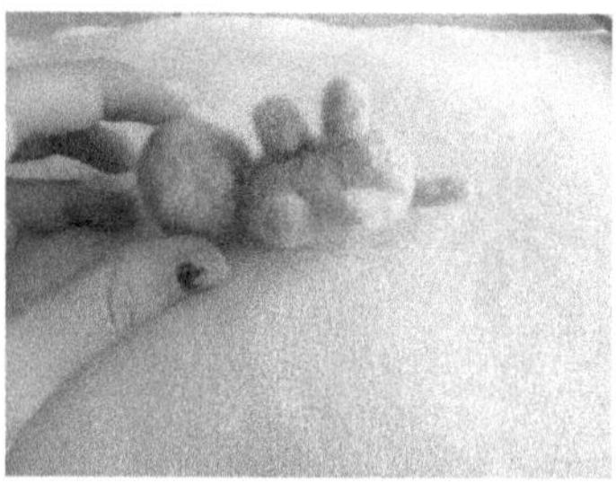

1. Roll a piece of wool tightly in your fingers. Stab it repeatedly. For a swirly tail, you can swirl with your fingers and stab the curved parts. Then, connect it to the back of the cat.

Make the Eyes and Ears

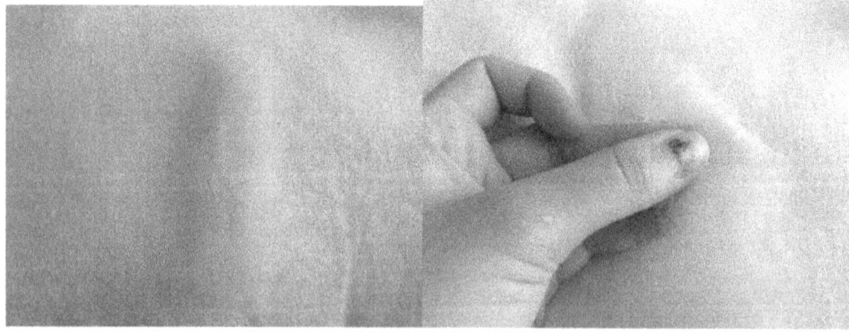

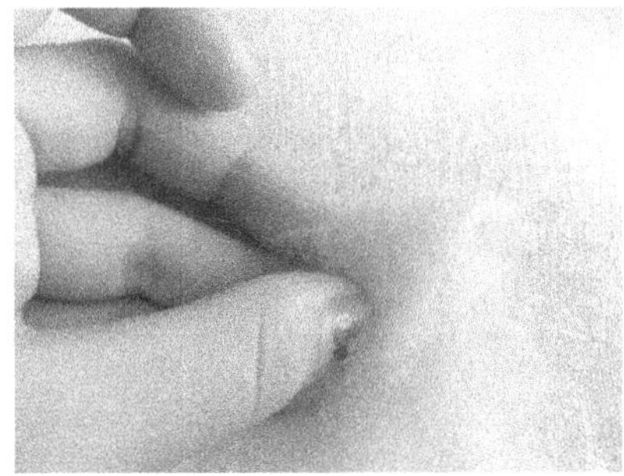

1. Get two strips of wool separately and fold into triangles. Cut them down to make them neat and attach to the head.

2. For the eyes, roll the black felting wool very tightly. Fix them to the front of the head.

Make the Pattern

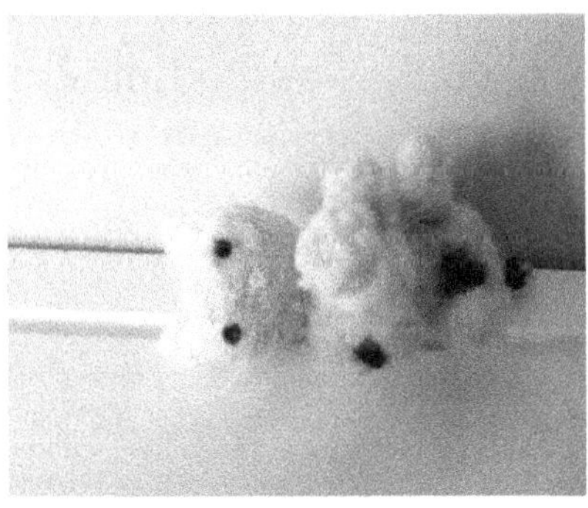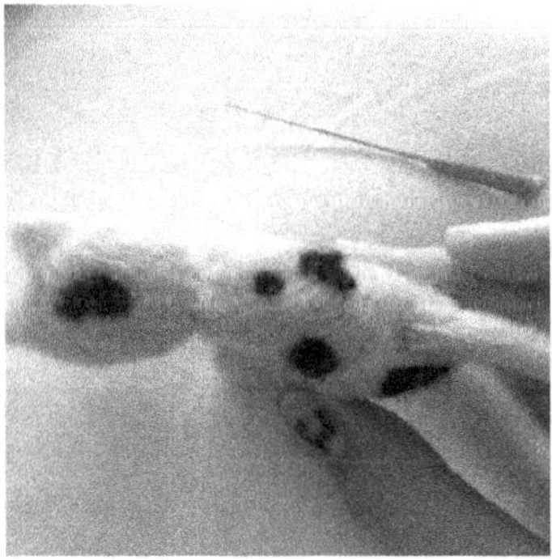

1. You can add your dots or stripes here for the finishing touch.

Mini Teacup Pincushion

This is a project that is perfect for a beginner in needle felting. You can make a set for your children. You can also use it to decorate your house. You can also gift it as well.

Let's get started

Things You Need:

- 20g merino wool roving for the cup and saucer (M)
- Small amounts of merino wool roving for the drink
- Small amounts of merino wool roving for the decoration
- Two size 40 triangular needles and a holder
- Embroidery needle
- A felting mat to work on
- Embroidery thread
- Finished teacup size: 4 x 8cm
  Finished saucer size: 8cm

Direction

1. Get a length of roving, of dimensions 50 x 4cm. Gently, make a flat strip from it and then roll to make a small tube. Start shaping the teacup with the two needles. Press one end when working, make it smaller and turn as you continue, to ensure the cup is round.

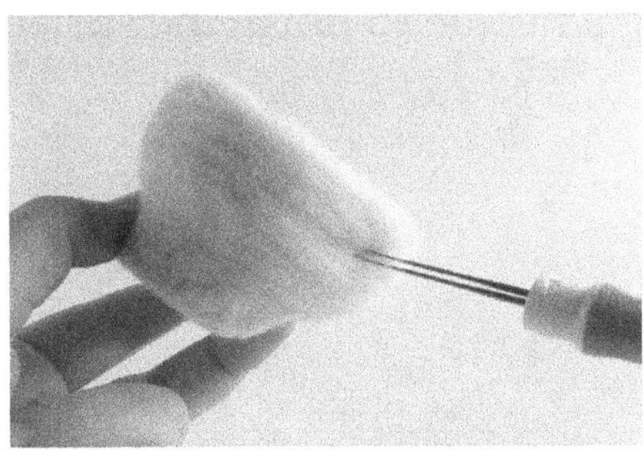

2. After forming the teacup, get tiny wool and create a small handle. You can first form it on your felting mat before fixing it to the cup.

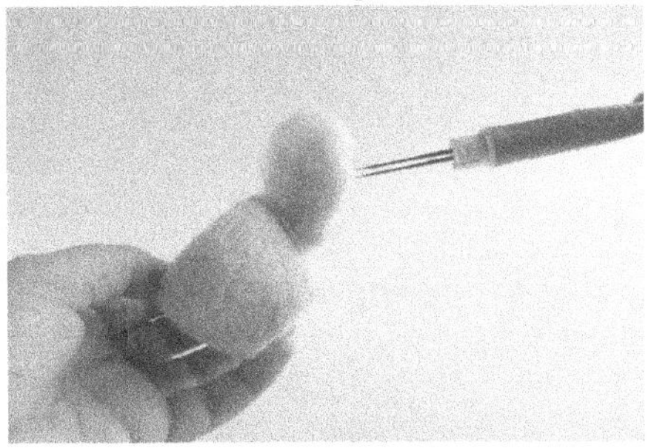

3. Create a decorative edge with a needle.

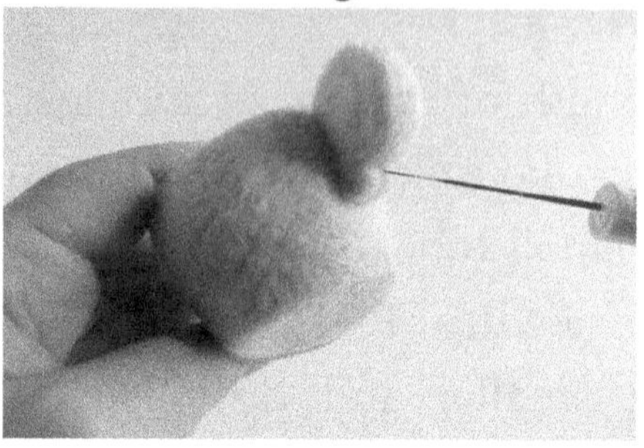

4. Neatly cover up the cup with a little wool layer, using a needle to finish the surface.

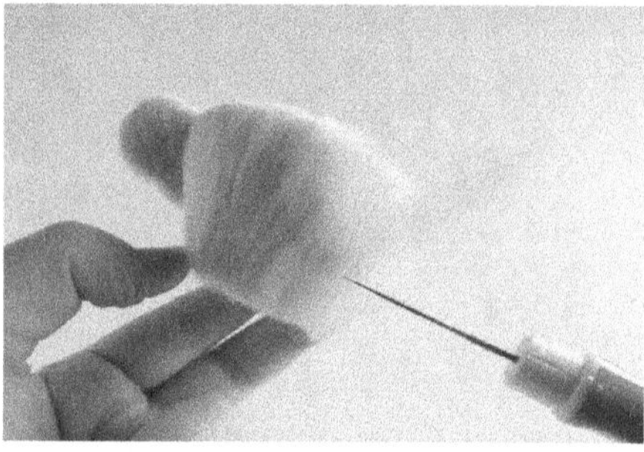

5. Needle felt your beverage wool to the top of the cup. Turn the wool in a round direction as you continue working.

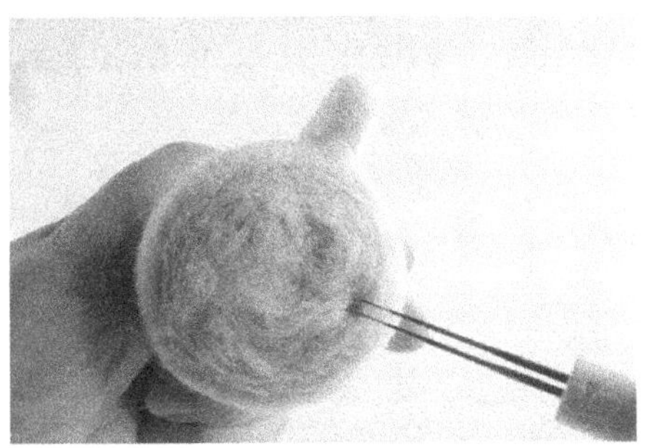

6. You can add the pattern on the surface. You can add a flowery effect by using a needle and tiny wools to add roses and leaves. Leave it loose and free so that it will look like hand-painted porcelain. Also, you can use bead for the surface pattern or use embroidery directly on the felt.

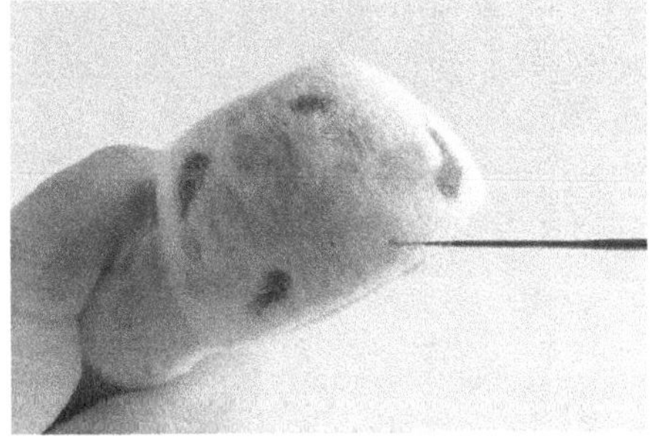

7. If you want to create the saucer, get a length of roving 30 x 4cm in length. Roll the roving to a saucer shape and work with two needles. Rotate it frequently to get a good round shape. Grasp the

edge upwards when you work to have a raised rim.

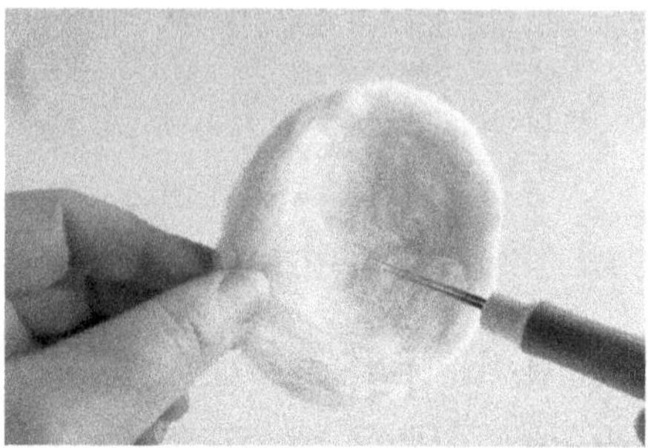

8. As the saucer becomes 8cm in diameter, cover with a thin layer of wool like you did for the cup. Then, sew plain stitching around the rim and inside the edge of the cup handle.

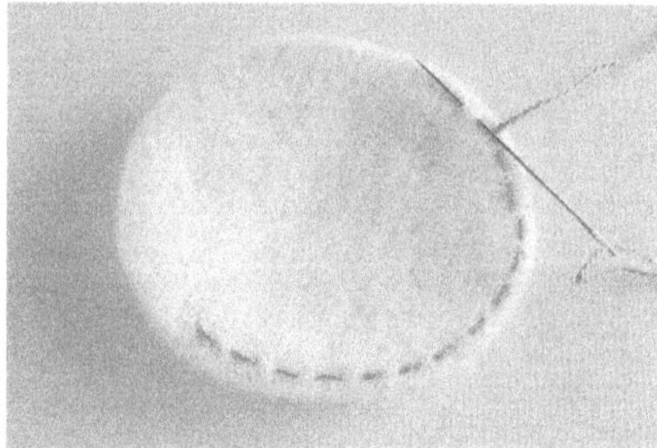

Felted Christmas Ornament

This is a delightful project you can work on during Christmas to decorate your homes and offices. You can also gift it to families and friends during the Christmas season.

Things You Need:

- A felting mat
- Roving
- Various needle holder
- At least 3-sized 40 felting needles, triangular or spiral
- Beading needle and thread

Large Tree Materials

- Red roving, 25 x 2cm
- 1m of trace gold chain
- 2 x green roving, 50 x 4cm
- Different colous of 8mm and 4mm beads
- Colorful assortment of 8mm and 4mm beads
- Tree size: 12cm, 7cm diameter at the base

Medium Tree Materials

- Cream or Ivory roving (2), 30 x 4cm
- 10mm red glass heart bead
- Red roving, 20 x 2cm

- 2 x ivory or cream roving, 30 x 4cm
- 21 x 4mm red glass heart beads
- Tree size: 9cm, Diameter at the base: 4.5cm

Small Tree Materials

- Red roving, 15 x 1cm
- 40 x red seed beads
- 2 x green roving, 15 x 3cm
- Finished Tree size: 6cm, Base Diameter: 4cm

Direction

1. Take out the fibers of one length and fold to form a tall triangular shape. Repeat with the other trees.

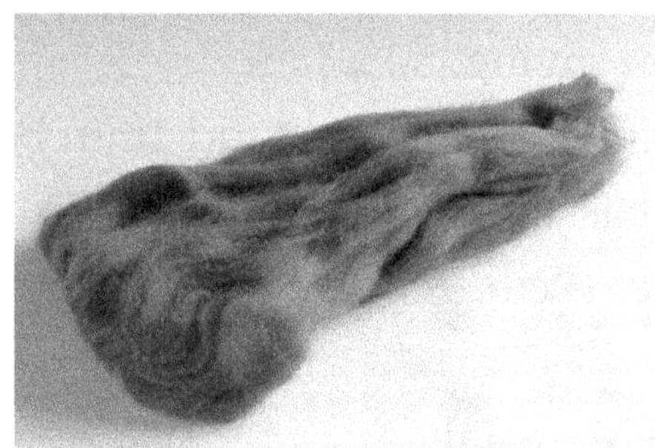

2. Get the other length of wool and roll to a ball. Then put inside the triangle to give it a fatter end

narrowing to an end like a carrot. Draw the corners of the outer wool to cover the filling.

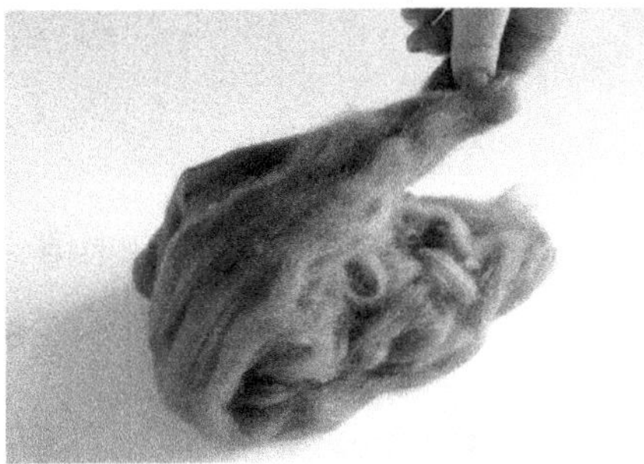

3. Start giving it a cone shape. For large trees, you can use three needles for speed. You can also use two needles.

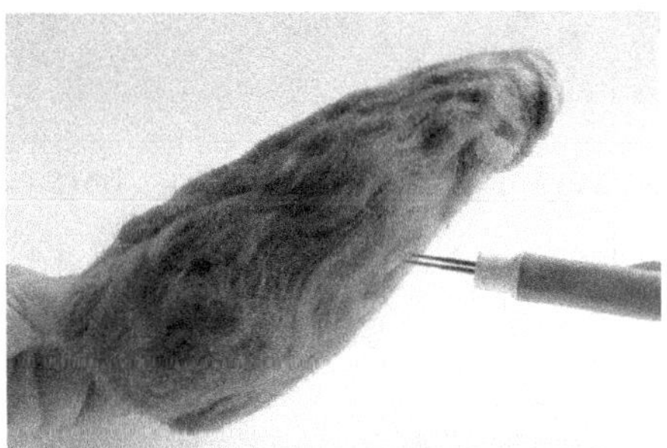

4. Continue to turn your tree as you work so that you can get an even roundness.

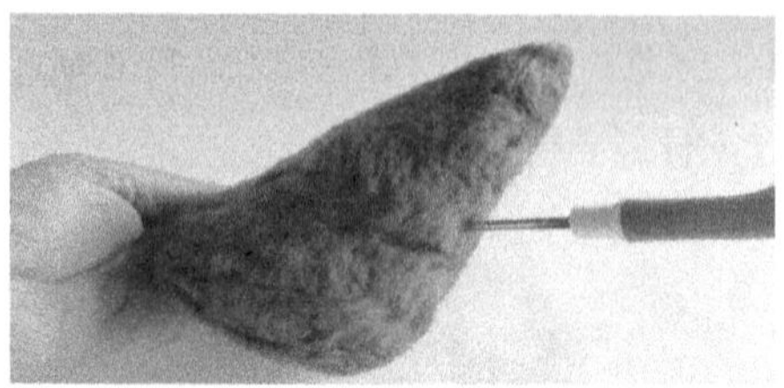

5. Hold the wool firmly with the cup of your forefinger and thumb when you shape the flat bottom.

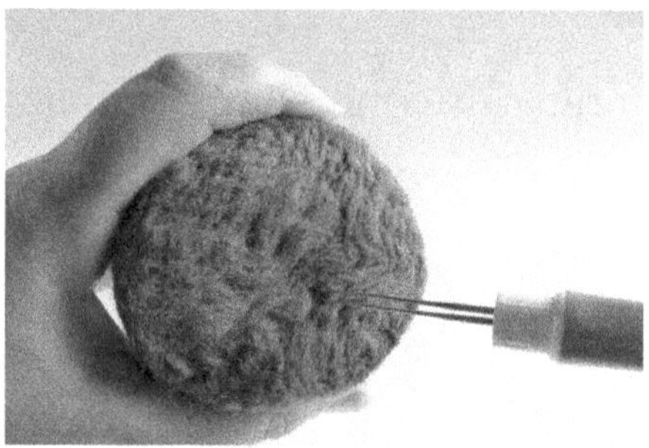

6. Press the wool together at the top of the tree and carefully use one needle to make a fine point.

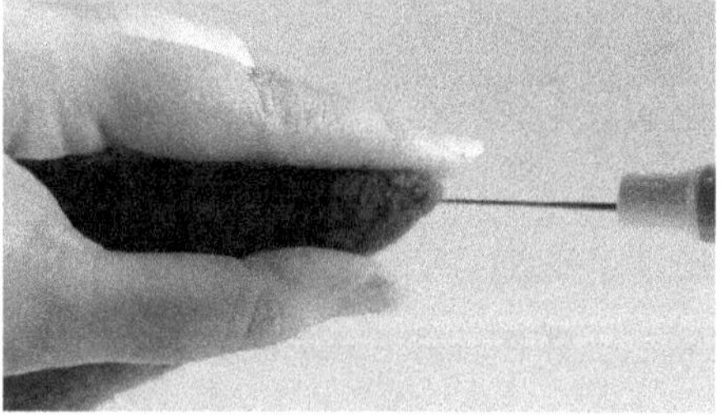

7. After your tree is dense and well formed, you can get thin layers of wool and cover a neat surface

on it, for a neat, uniform finish. You can begin
with two needles and finish with one.

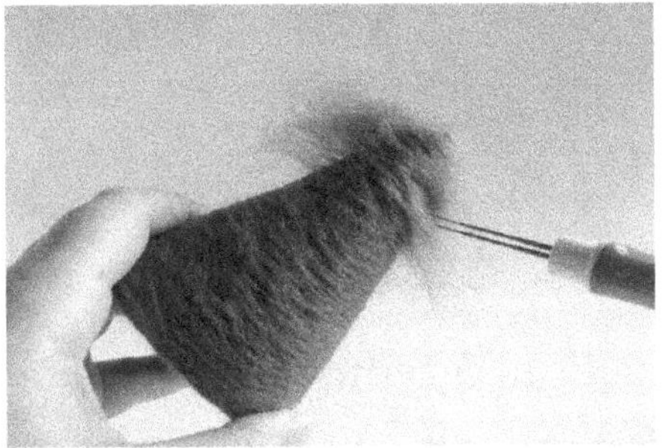

8. Envelop the tree's base with the length of red
   wool and needle it securely to form a base. Fold
   any remaining wool under the tree bottom.

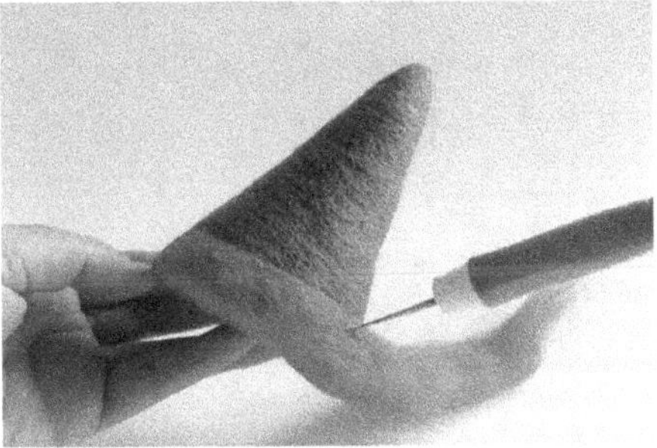

9. With your pins, mark and measure the place your
   trimmings will be fixed.

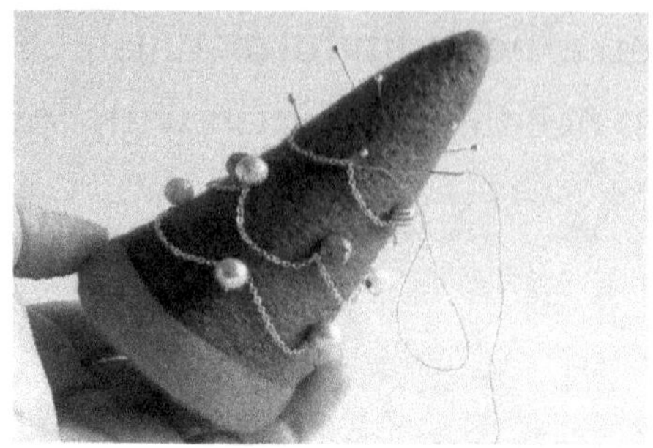

10. After positioning your beads, sew them on using a beading needle. You can use as many bead baubles as you want to get people into the festive spirit.

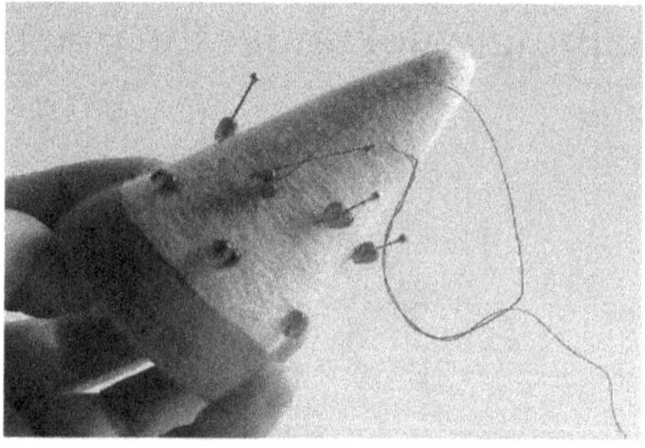

Your Felted Christmas Tree is ready!

Felted Fox

Things You Need:

- Wool roving of different colors (white, orange and dark brown)
- Felting needle
- Felting pad
- Wool felt sheets, tan and dark brown.
- Needle and brown thread
- 2 blue buttons
- Fabric glue

Optional

- Pipe cleaners
- Mini quilting iron
- High gloss decoupage medium

Direction

1. Create the head and body of the fox.

   Start by putting a handful of orange wool roving on your felting pad. Ruffle it and fold the wool to a medium-sized zucchini shape, narrowing one corner of the wool mass. With a barbed felting needle, start stabbing the needle carefully into the wool in slow strokes. Hold your wool against the felting pad so that the needle will pass through the wool into your protective pad instead of stabbing your own flesh.

Keep stabbing the wool in an up and down direction all through the wool's pointed end, till the fibers being entangled ends up becoming stiff. Fold the wool fiber to form a soft, elbow-like shape; then, use the needle to felt the face and the body of the fox uniformly.

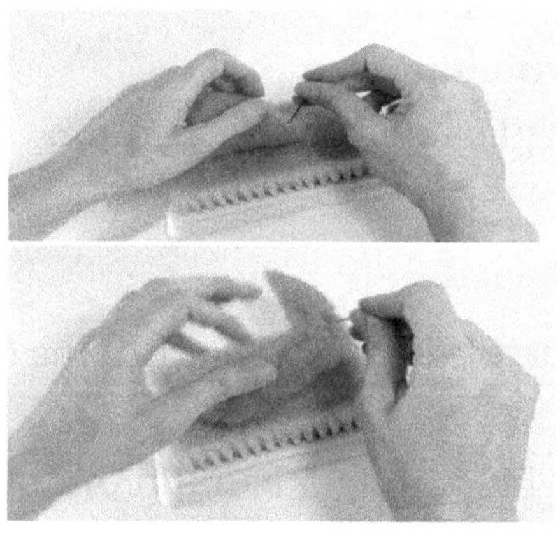

There are diverse fiber lengths and thicknesses in wool roving, even though some packages do not clearly state the kind of roving inside. When your roving is good and free from any foreign specks, it means that it has been carded more than the wool used for this project and may require more felting than the one shown in the example.

2. Keep Shaping the Fox's Body

After getting a uniformly matted elbow shape with one pointed end, get a handful of your white wool roving and smoothen the wool to a tube shape that is akin to the orange wool's length. Keep the orange shape apart for a while, and begin to stab the felting needle into the white wool roving to tangle the fibers together.

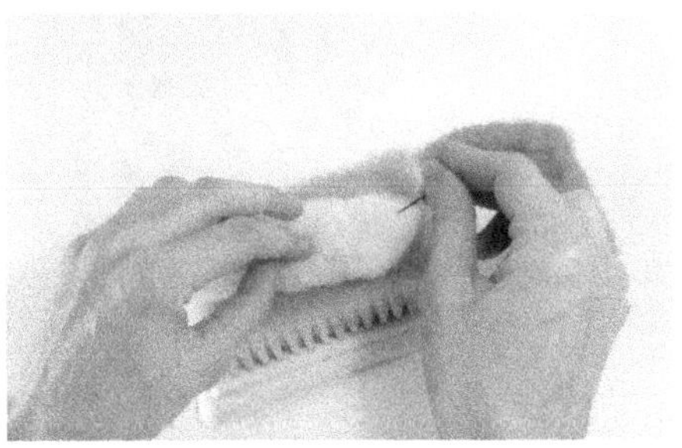

When the white wool becomes uniformly consistent, place the white wool against the orange wool's inner curvature. Push the white and orange roving on your felting pad, white side up, stab through the white wool and the orange wool with the barbed needle so that you will entangle the fibers and fix the two colors.

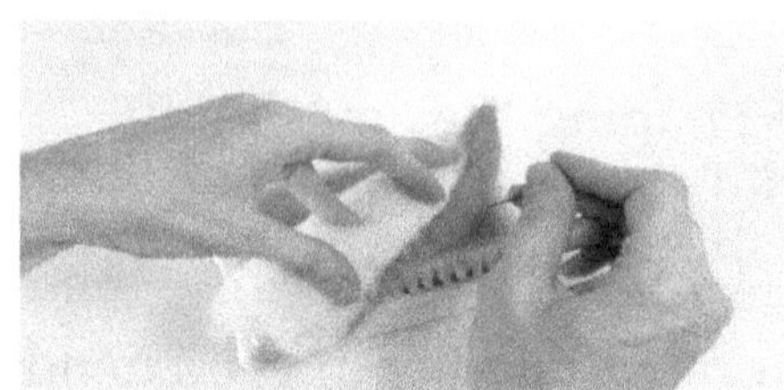

Keep jabbing the needle through the white and orange wool until you get a shape that looks like the fox's tummy and head.

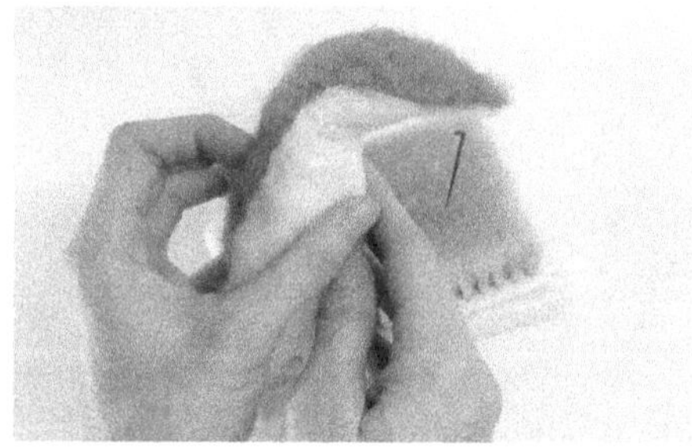

3. Confirm the Size of the Button Eyes

This is time to compare your blue bottom eyes next to the fox's head to confirm whether the size is right.

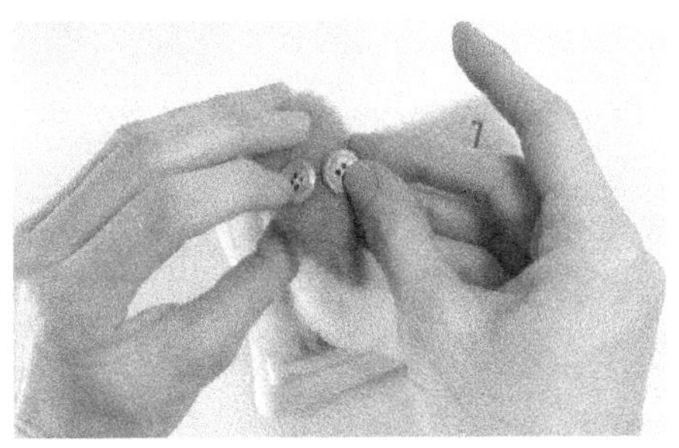

To make the body of your fox smaller, keep stabbing your project till the whole mass has been squeezed, or trim the excess materials with scissors. When the fox's body is too small, you can pull at the wool roving to increase or stretch it, then put more wool on your project and stab it with your barbed needle. Be careful of ridges and seams that you can create when patching a project. You can pull a little wool and felt it into the naturally occurring grooves that will help to give the project a faultless look. Keep patching the body of the fox till you get the right proportion.

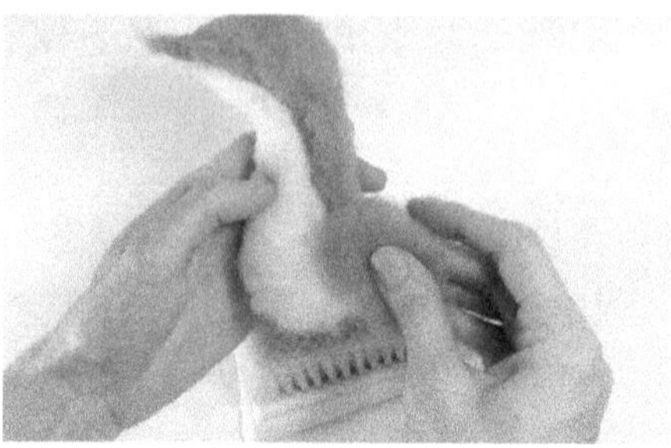

Remember that you cannot achieve perfection in needle felting, but you may want to continue patching.

4. Make the Arm and Leg Limbs

Draw a thin length of wool roving, and felt the wool with the barbed needle till you have a fox limb that is approximately the length and width of an index finger. Cover the end of the fox limb with a little amount of brown felt to create a paw and jab it with the needle to attach the orange and brown wool.

To create limbs that have more structure, you can begin by covering the roving around a piece of craft grade pipe cleaner. Then you can continue to felt the limbs.

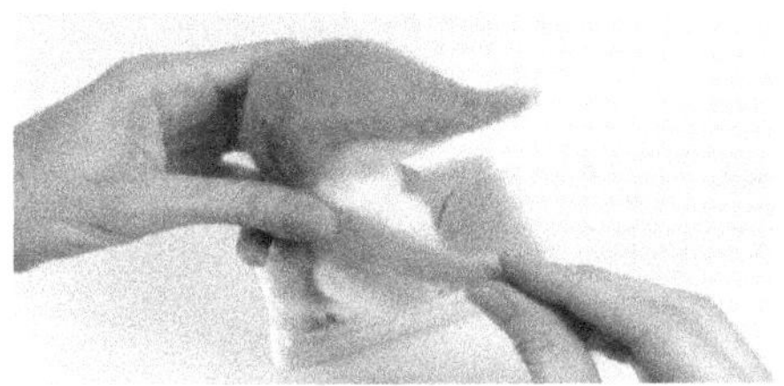

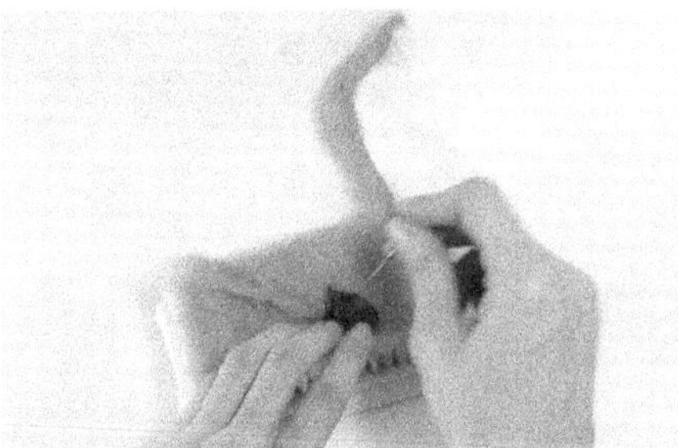

After completing the arm of the fox, keep it on the body of the fox, where the shoulder is positioned, and stab the wooly end with your barbed needle till the wool becomes firmly attached.

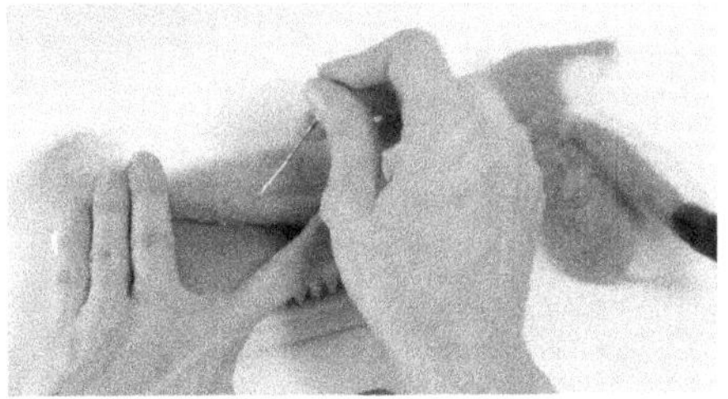

Create the second arm of the fox, which is of the same size as the first arm, and attach to another side of the fox's body. Then, create two slightly shorter limbs for the hind limbs and fix to the body also.

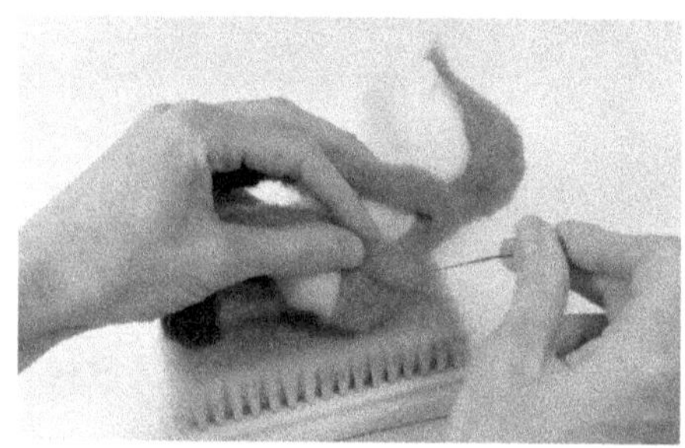

5. Make the Tail

Take a bundle of orange wool roving that is almost the size of the body. Fix one end, however, leave the remaining mass free.

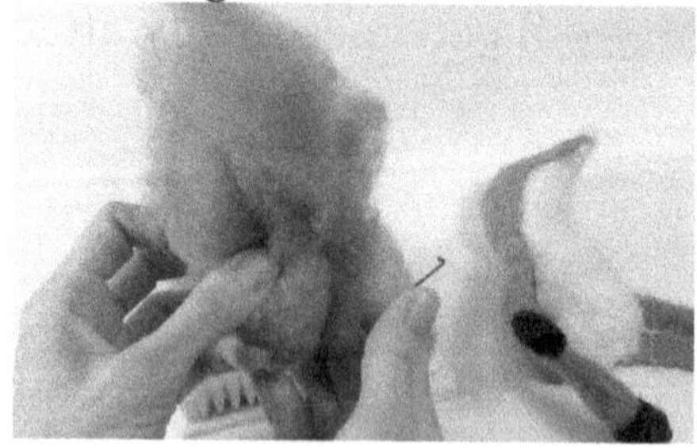

Needle the wool mass till it looks like an ice cream cone and is thick enough to hold together as you tug at it.

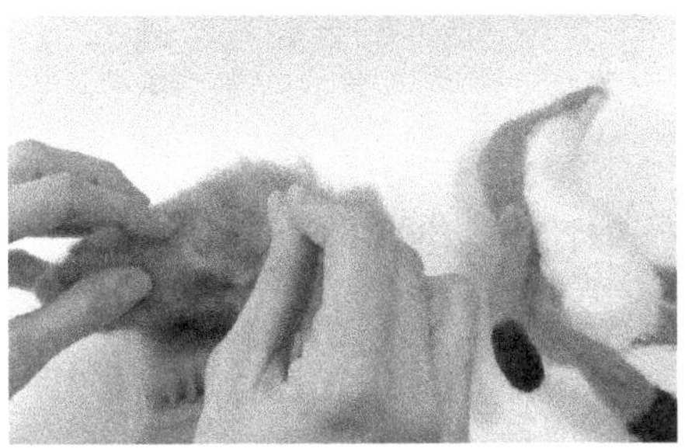

Take small white roving and felt to the extreme end of the orange ice cream cone shape. Keep shaping the tail with your needle till the piece becomes flawless.

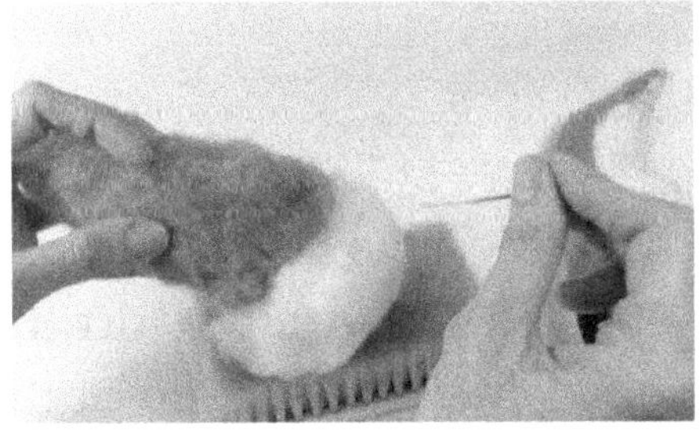

Fix the tail of the fox to its back. Patch the tail with an extra piece of wool roving.

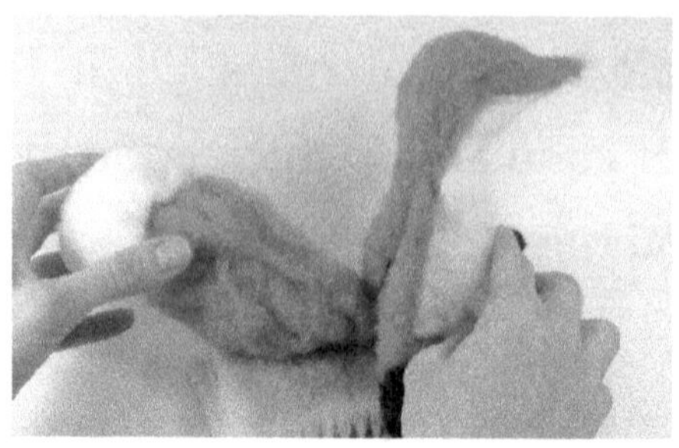

6. Sew on the Eyes to Position

Sew on the eye buttons on the face with your needle and thread. You can conceal your thread now underneath one of the buttons.

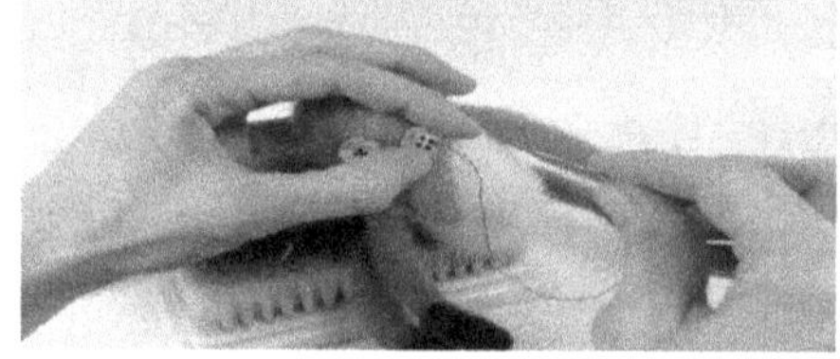

7. Make the Nose

Attach a little wool roving to the tip of the fox's nose and felt it securely. Turn the brown roving before keeping it on the tip of the nose. Twisting the fibers before you set them against the remaining piece will help you make a cleaner line when you start felting it.

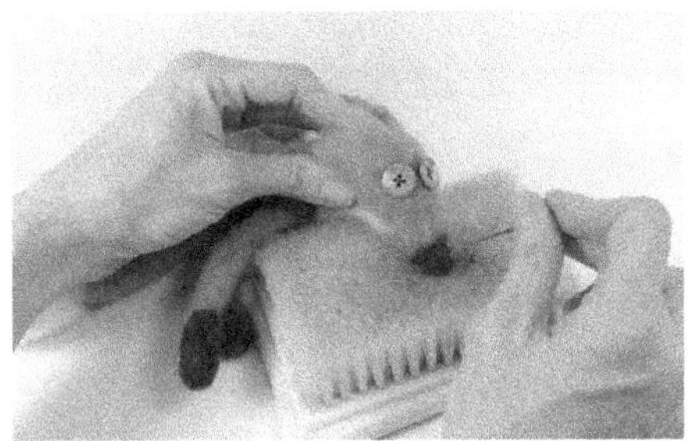

8. Create the Ears

For the fox's ears, cut two oval shapes from brown felt sheets. Also, cut two slightly smaller than ovals from wool felt. Note that the ears are big; therefore, you need to cut bigger ovals than you assume you need. It is easier to cut away excess than to add more.

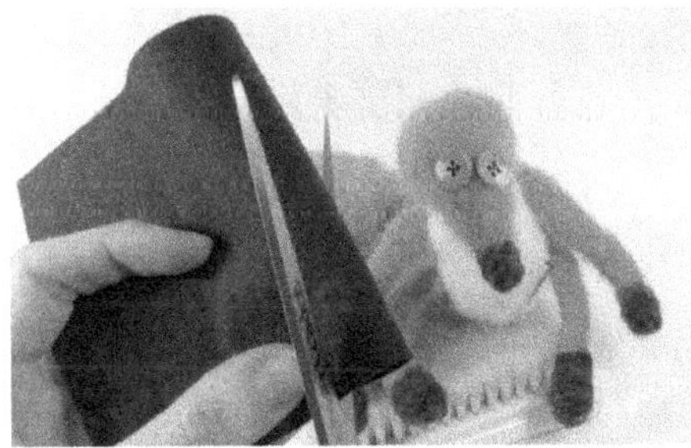

Stitch the ears in position on the head of the fox with the needle and thread. Use fabric glue to patch the inner tan ovals. Leave the glue to totally dry.

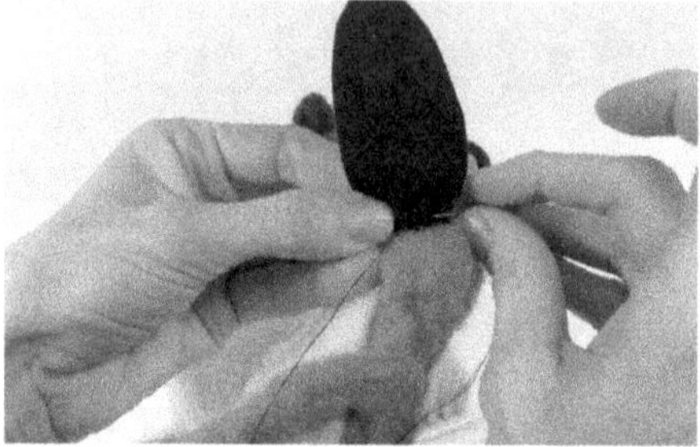

Sewing felt fox ears to a needle felted fox body.

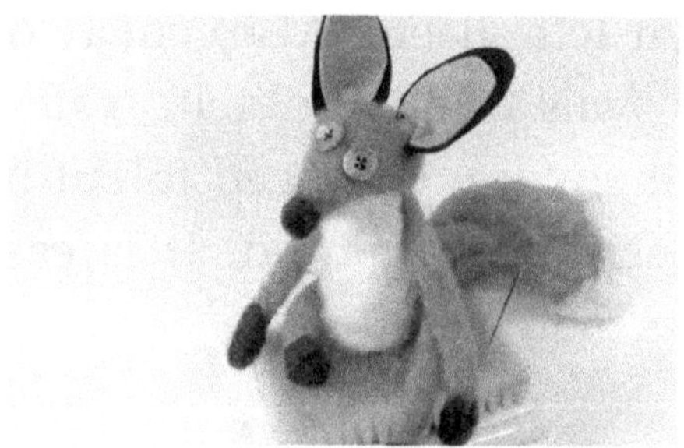

9. Give the Fox a Detailed Finish

You might need to add accents in the tail by stabbing the needle in even rows to make intentional lines, or you may need to fix roving patches for added bulk in specific areas.

If you want to reduce the strands to a minimum, cut with sharp scissors or press with a hot iron. The heat from the iron will smoothen the fox and finish it.

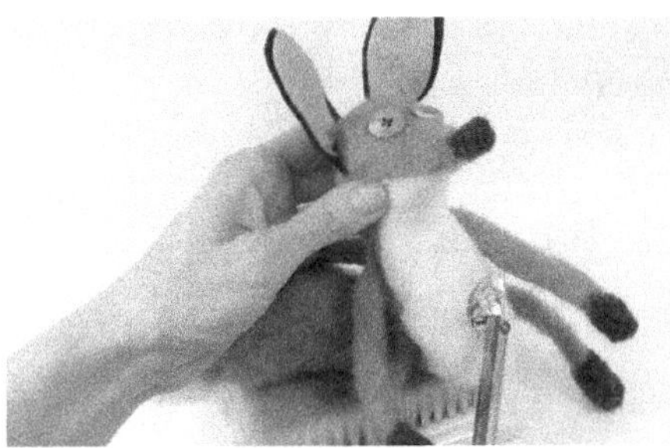

You can add more details to the fox's eyes by applying a coat of high gloss decoupage medium to the buttons.

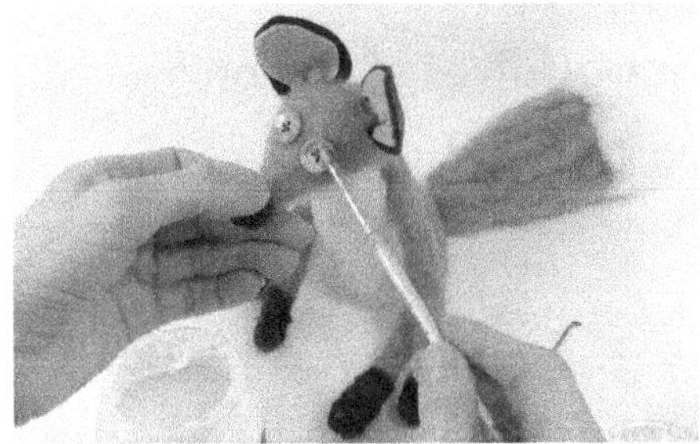

Felted Rabbit

This is another 3 Dimensional animal project. With enough practice and patience, you can create it as well.

Things You Need:

- Wool roving (color: beige, orange, green and pink)
- Felting needles
- Sponge
- Two beads
- Thread
- Needle handle
- Sewing needles

Direction

1. Create the Basic Parts

Place a handful of wool on the sponge. Wrap it tightly with your fingers.

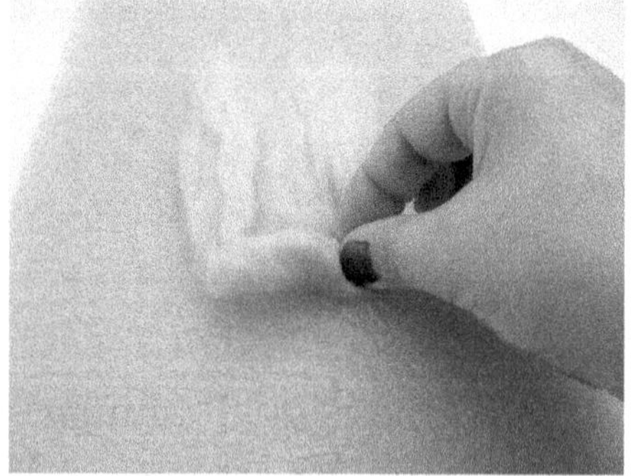

After wrapping for several times, bend the edges in and continue wrapping.

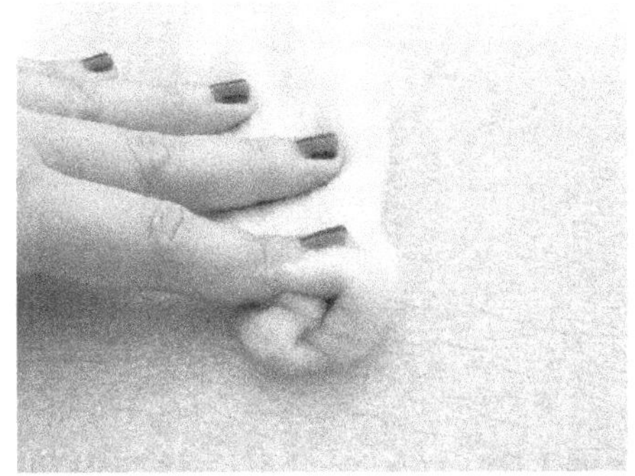

Keep the wool tight and put all the ends inside the ball.

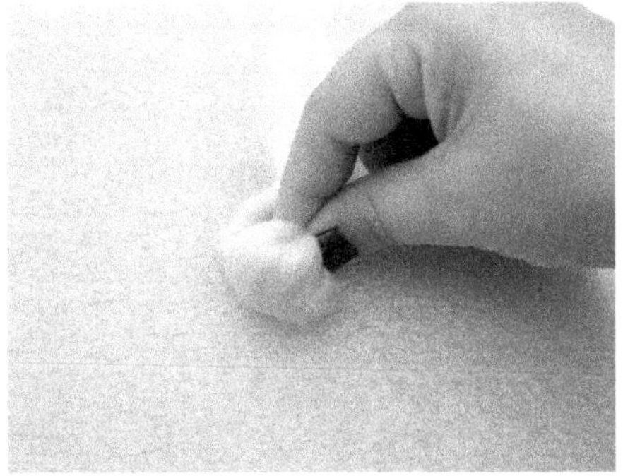

Continue punching it. With more punches to the wool, the shape will become solid and take a form.

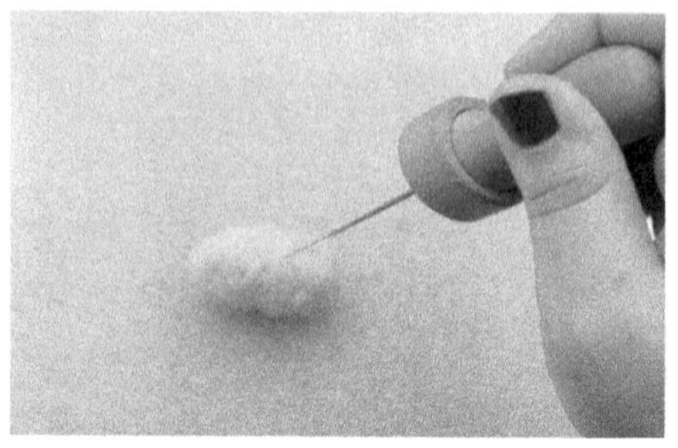

This will be the body of the rabbit. Initially, it will be fluffy and rough, but it will take form with time. You need to get a bean-like shape.

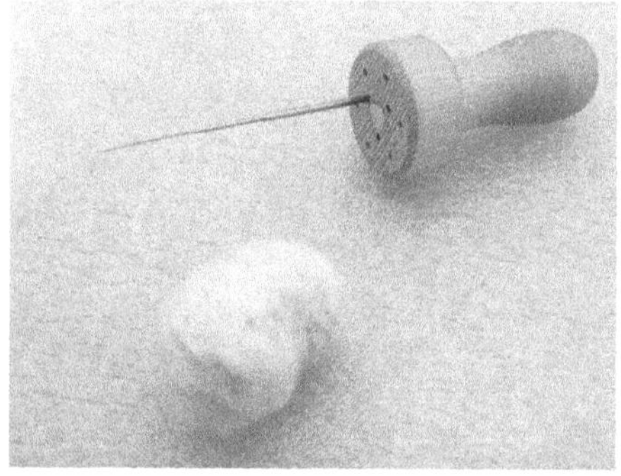

Repeat the previous steps to create a small ball that will serve as the head.

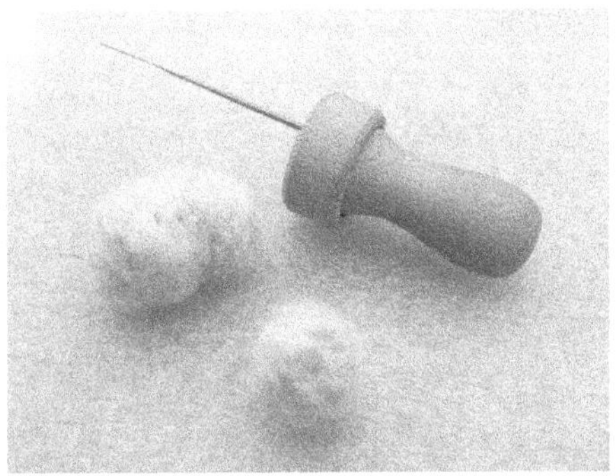

2. Felt the Snout

Take a small bundle of fibers from the rove and divide it into two.

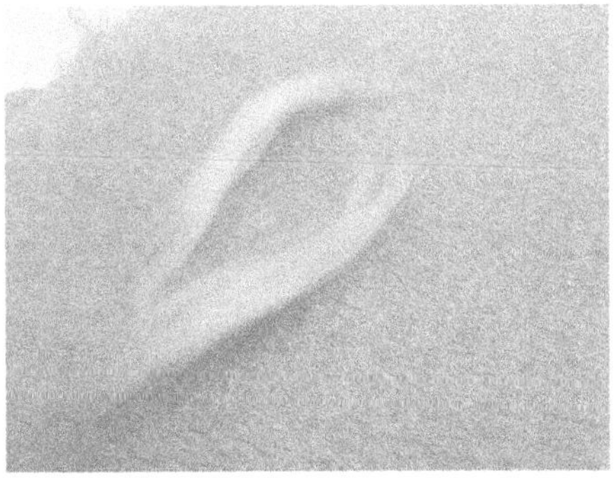

Fold the fibers to create two small balls of the same size

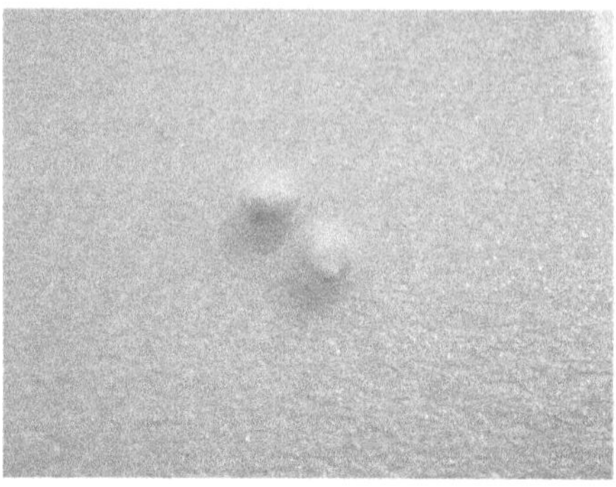

Keep them on the head ball and attach to the head with the needle

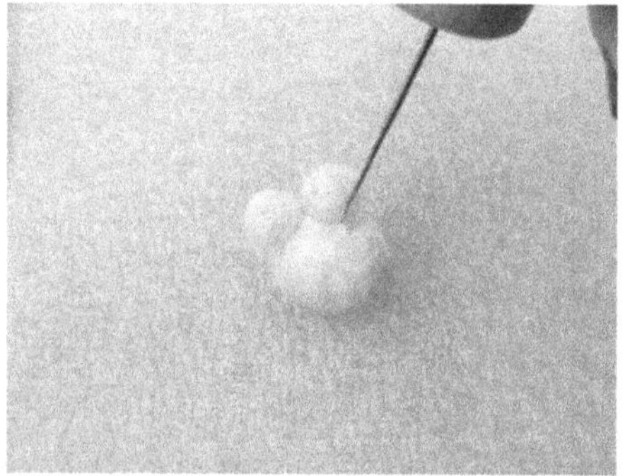

Form a little triangle by stabbing on the sponge. Draw a small amount of pink fibers and fold the triangle.

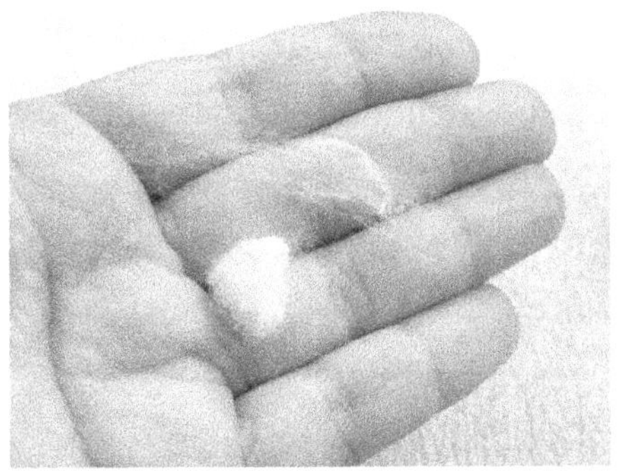

Keep it on the two balls. It will be the nose.

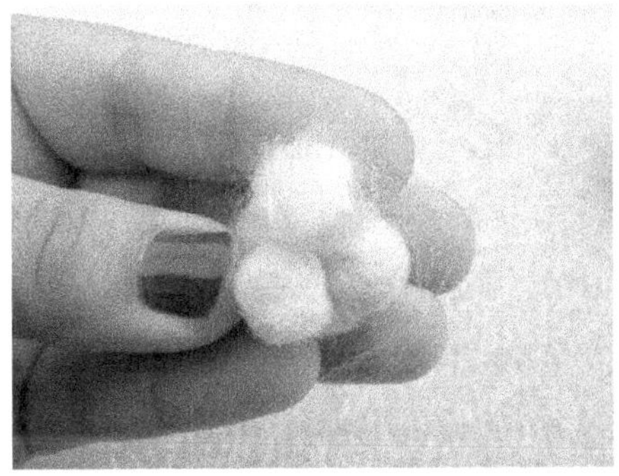

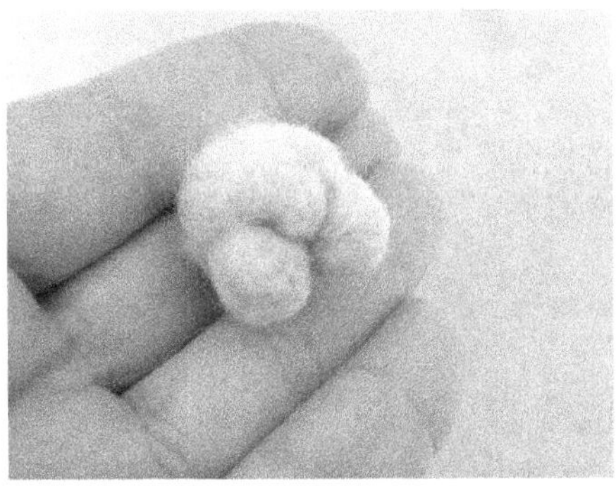

3. Make the Face

Continue felting the small pieces and add to the face. Keep one piece on both sides of the snout to create the cheeks.

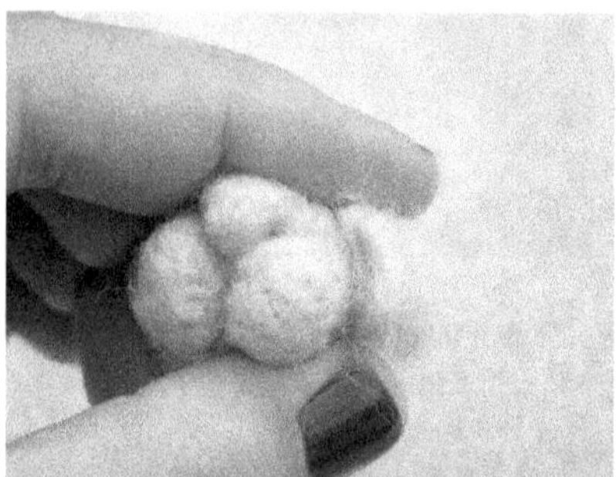

Now, you don't need to spend much time on shaping. Just fix the pieces to get some volume and general shaping.

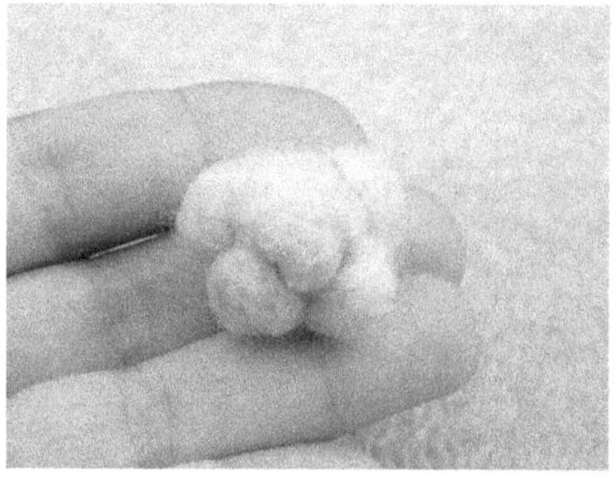

Stitch with the sewing needle. Use similar thread color as the bead. Make a stitch and position the first bead at eye height. Then, sew on the bead.

Pull the needle via the other side to keep the eyes in line.

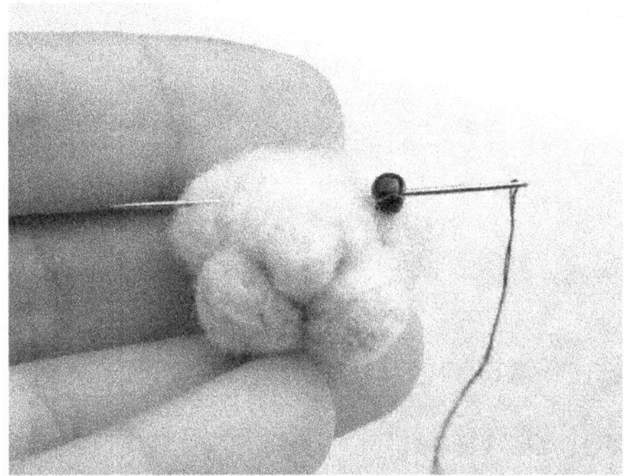

Use the second bead. Fix it in position and drag the needle through to the bottom of the head.

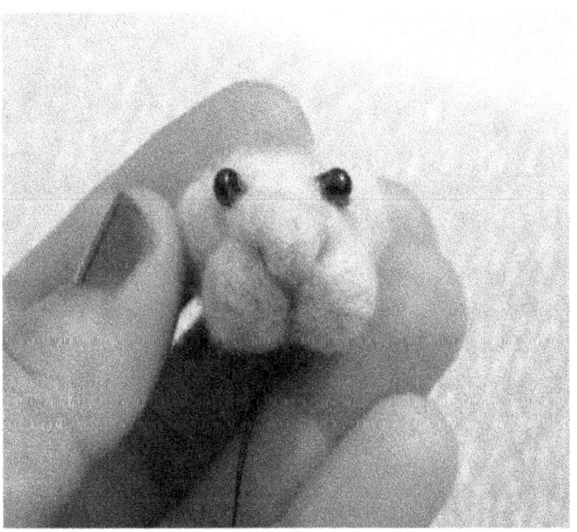

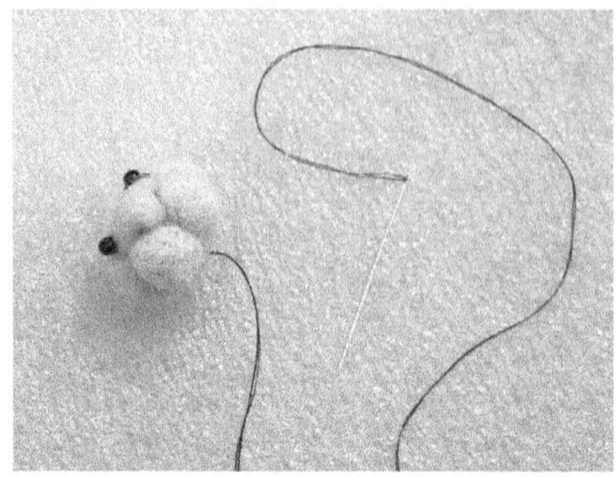

Secure the connection between the head and the body. Fret not at the different thread color. It will become covered in the end.

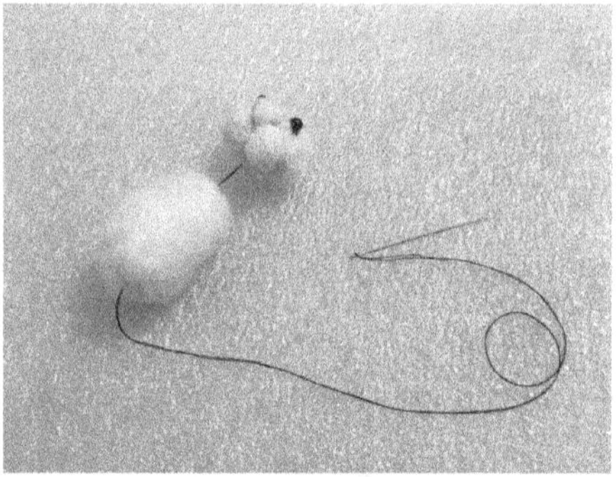

Tangle some fibers to create a small strip.

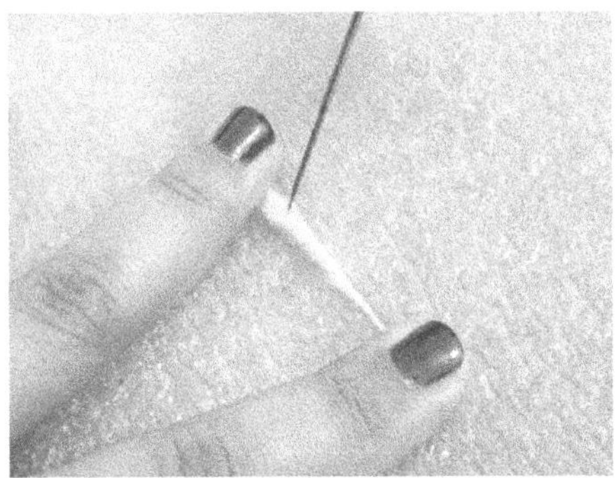

Position it at the eye area to create lower and upper eyelids.

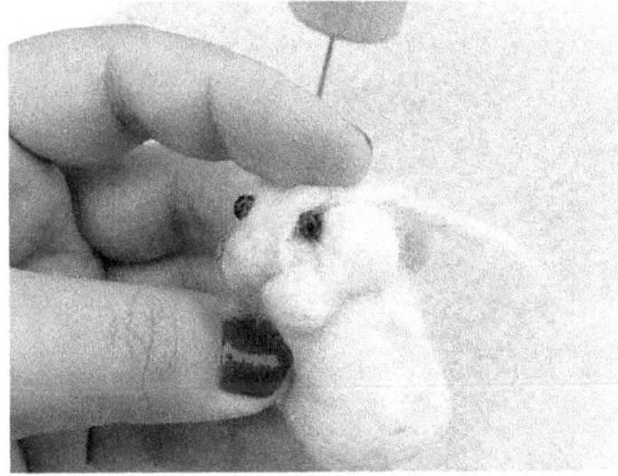

Connect the forehead and the nose with a piece. As the punches increase, it takes on a more uniform shape.

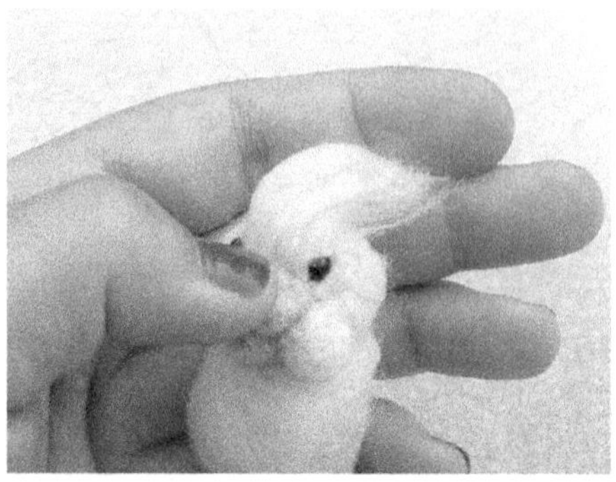

Add another small piece to make the mouth.

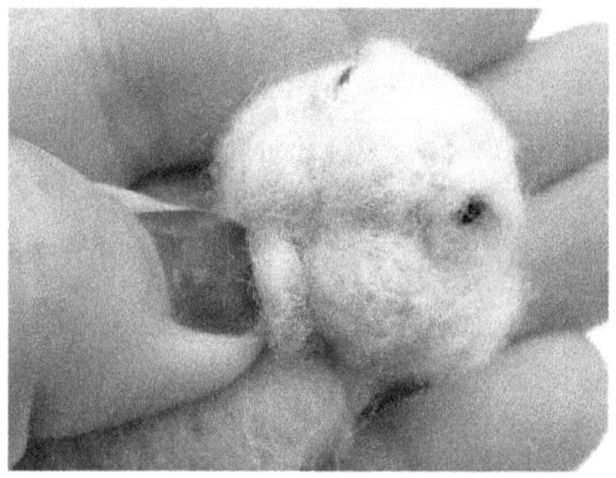

4. Create the Body Parts

   Create the front legs by felting two pieces. Make the back legs and feet with two bigger pieces.

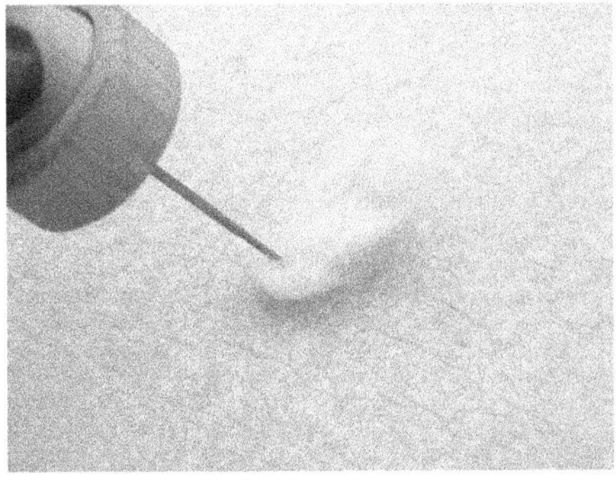

This is how the pieces will look like:

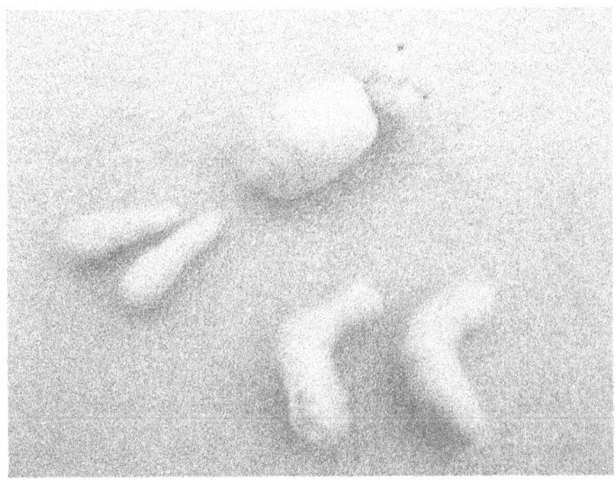

Draw a few fibers from the pink wool. Entwine them and keep on the edge of the front legs to make the toes. Take a small pink circle on the inner side to complete the paws.

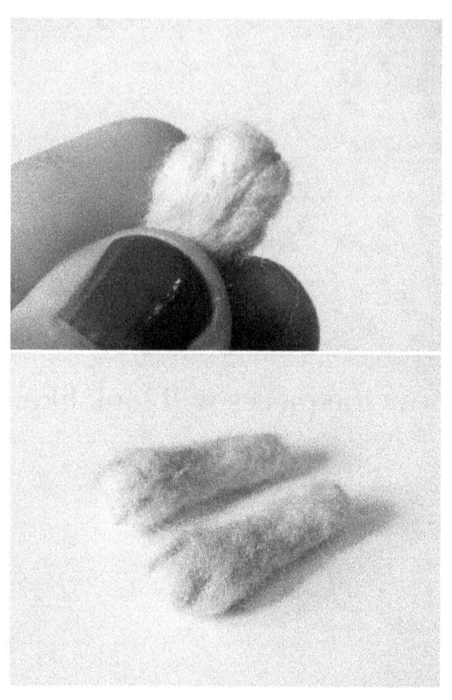

Do the same for the feet also.

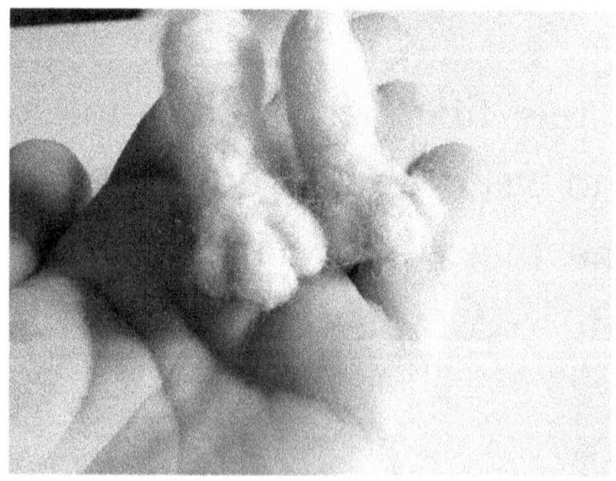

5. Finish Assembling the Body

Keep the arms in the rightful place and set them in place with the needle.

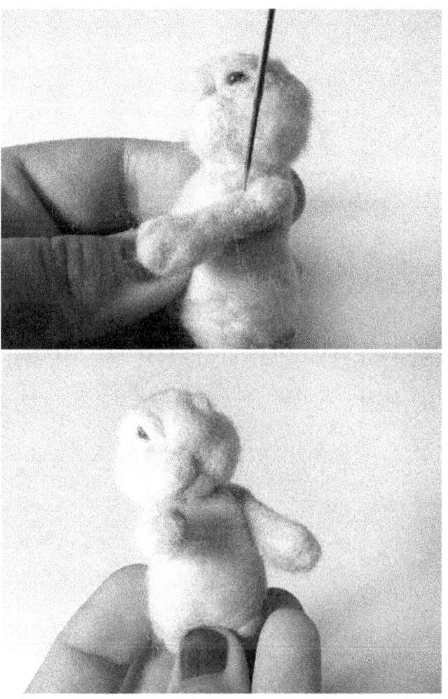

Repeat the steps for the legs.

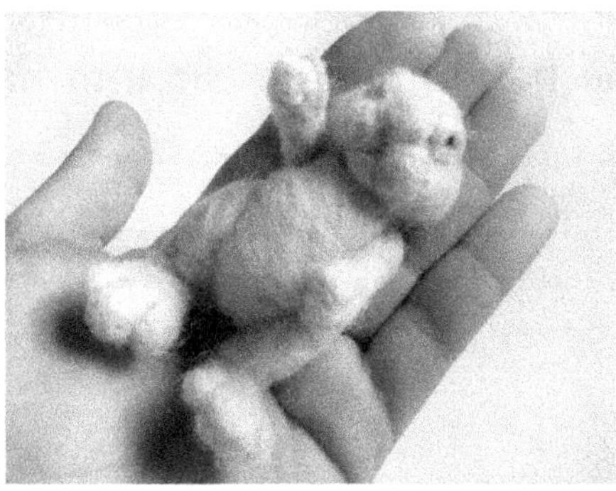

Create a triangular shape for the ears

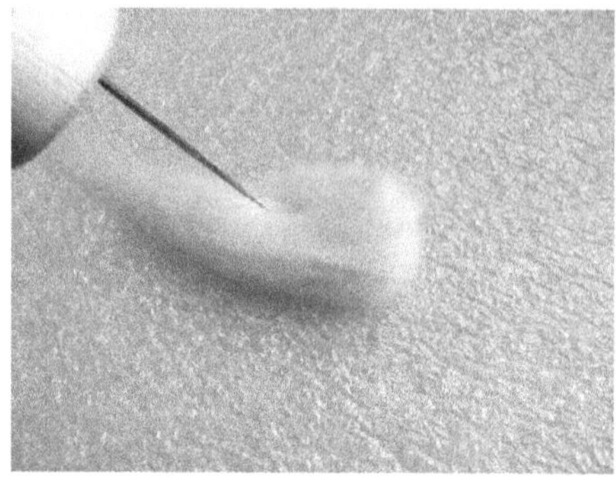

After getting the shape you desire, put some pink fibers inside the ear.

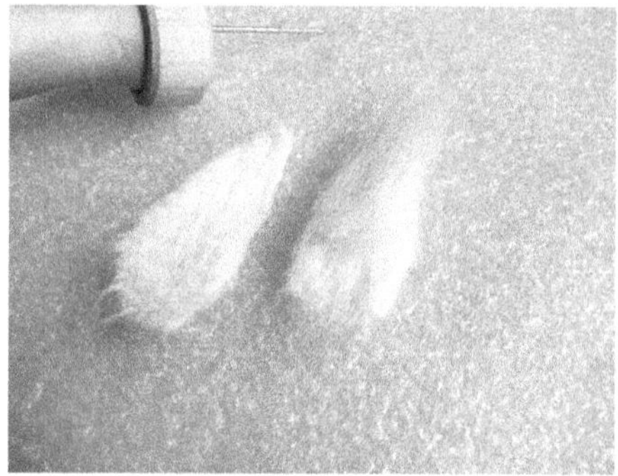

Bend the bottom of the ear into half and create some punches.

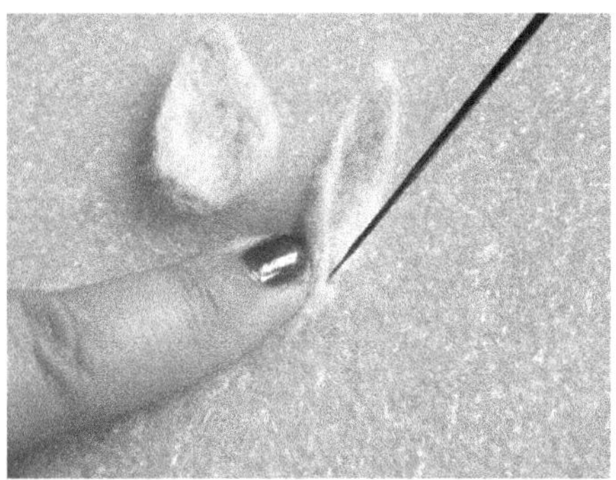

Fix the ears on the head of the rabbit.

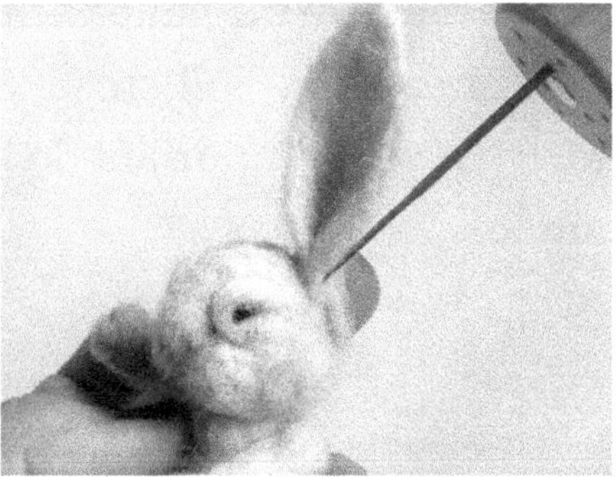

6. Final Details

   Now, you can add the final details punches. You can amend the shape of the eyelid, secure the parts, and amend the shape of the nose.

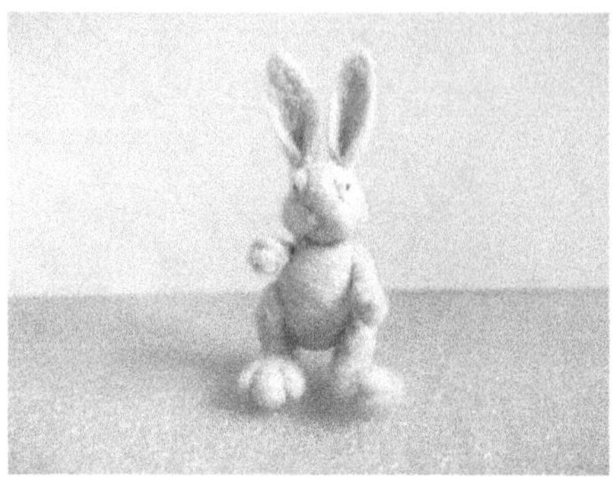

Include a few pink fibers here to add color and depth to your rabbit. You can punch continuously in particular areas that will create a deep line or hole, which is very important in making your rabbit unique.

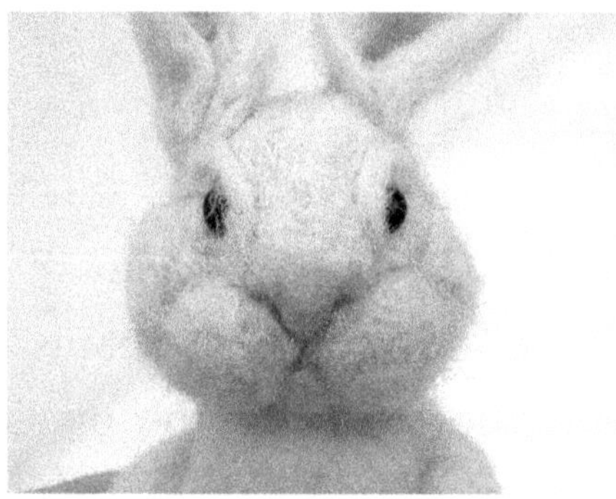

You can also increase the volume of some areas or add some pieces on top to remove any intense lines. Continue to punch to remove volume.

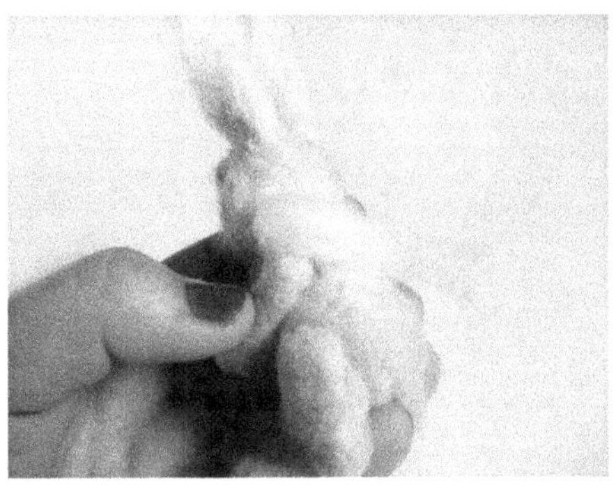

Finish up by adding the tail.

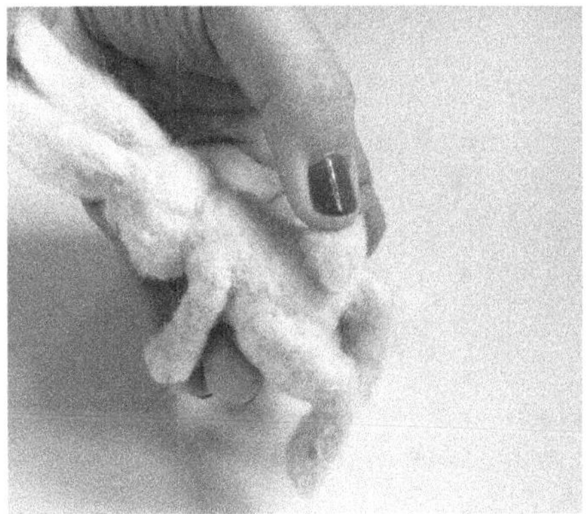

7. Make Your Rabbit Happy

Create a carrot with the orange wool

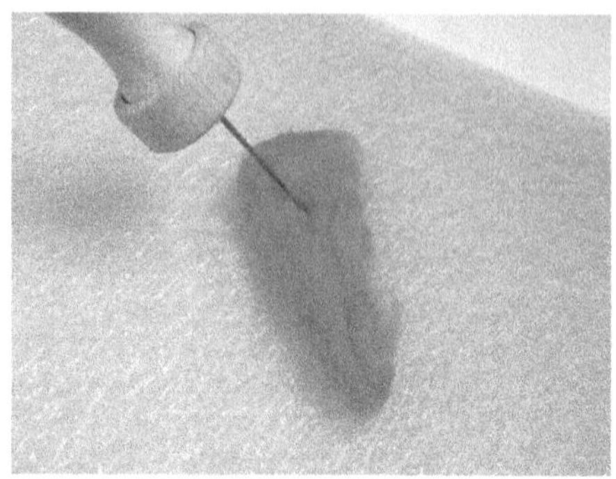

Continue to wrap new piece, wound it and stab to make the final shape

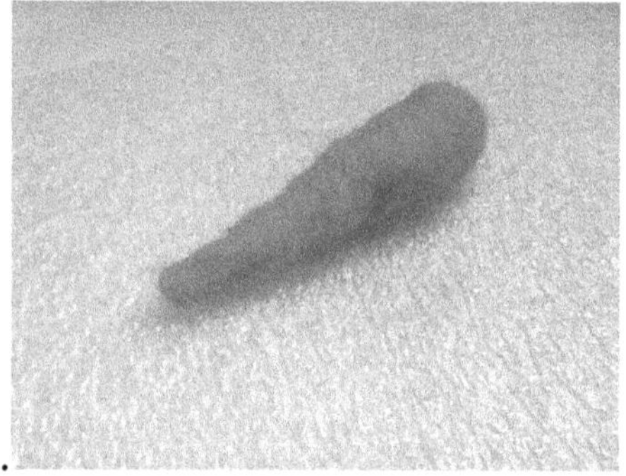

Create the carrot leaves with the green wool

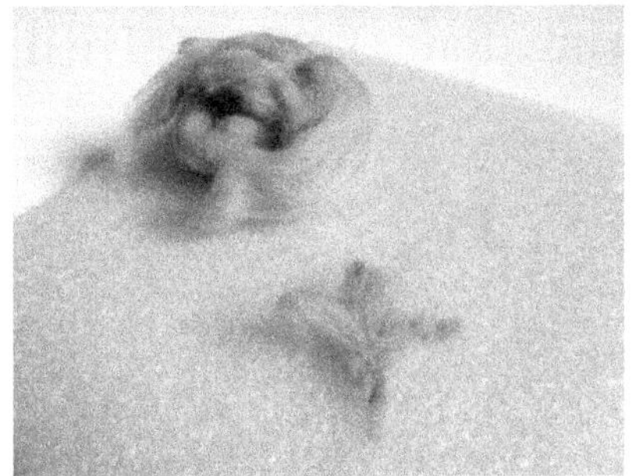

Connect to the carrot

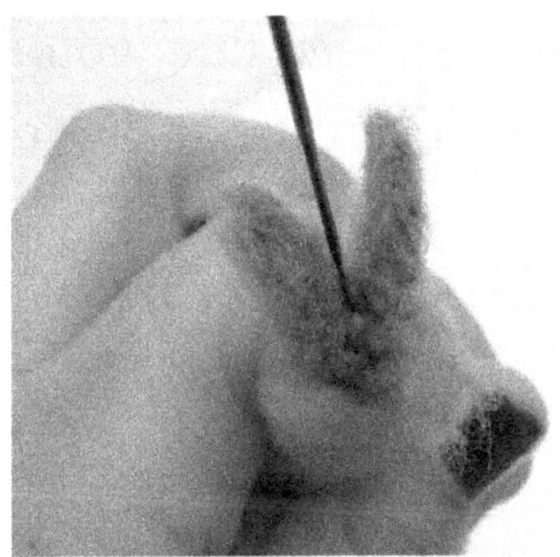

Give the rabbit and the carrot punch a hug.

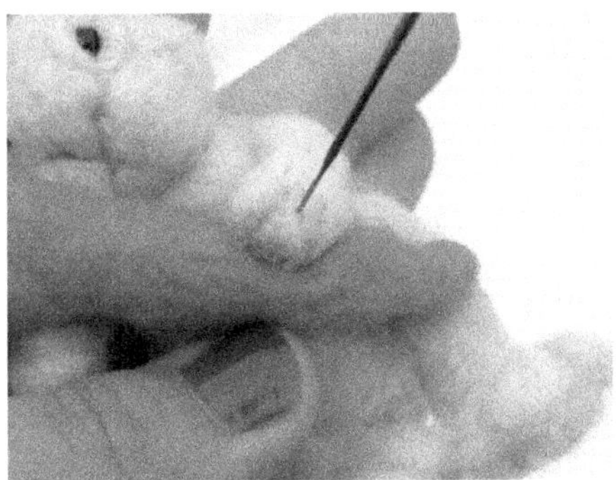

Now you are done. You can give it out as a gift.

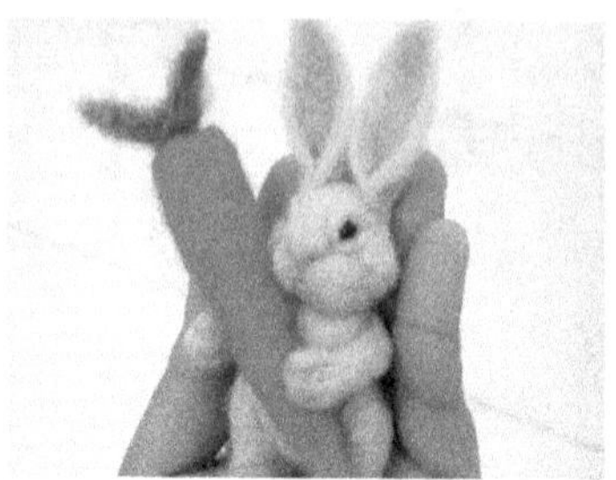

Felted Button

This is a very simple project that you can complete within a short time. You can use it on your clothes, or sell it to others.

Things You Need:

- Wool roving
- Felting needle
- Foam pad
- Wool Yarn

Direction

1. Shape some wool roving to a round flat disc of about 5cm diameter and 2cm thick.

2. As you continue stabbing the wool, it will become firm and reduce by one-third of the original size

3. Continue to jab the wool with the needle till it becomes firm and to the wanted size.

4. Jab the disc more in the middle to create the classic button shape.

5. Needle four small holes in the middle of the button to serve as a guide to sew the yarn through.

Felted Plants

This is an amazing 3-dimension project that involves both wet felting and needle felting. Here, it started with needle felting and ends with wet felting. This project requires some patience and practice.

Things You Need:

- Fine Merino wool 10g
- Carded Maori Wood
- Felting needle
- Foam rubber
- Warm water
- Soap
- Bubble wrap
- Scissors
- Thin foam sheet

Direction

1. Lay out a piece of foam rubber on your working surface and keep a 20cm circle of Merino wool layer on it.

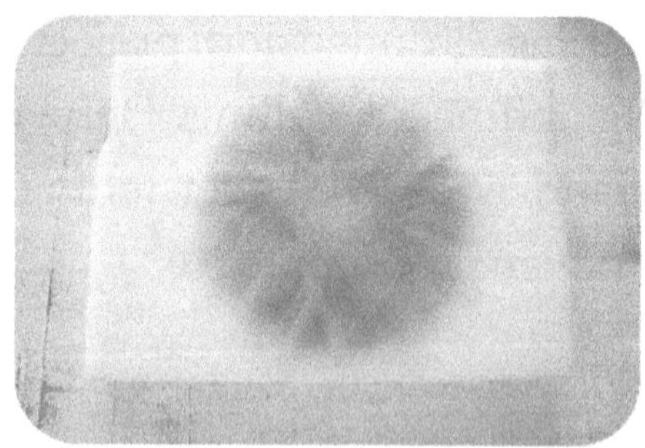

2. Place 2 layers of Maori on the Merino wool, close to the edge, leaving the center intact

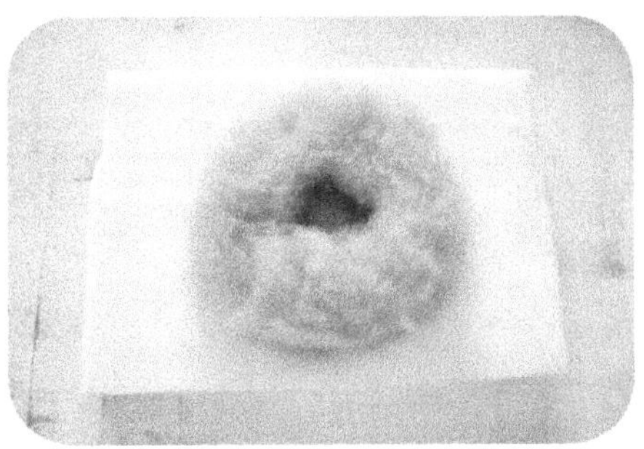

3. Cover up the surface with 2 layers of Merino wool again, like it is shown, in a spherical direction

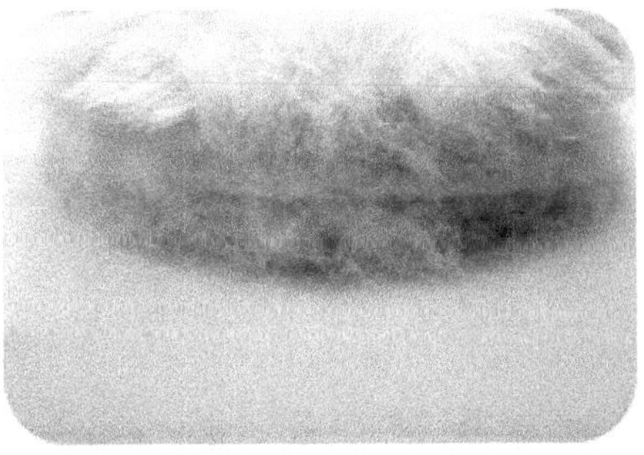

4. Place on the fiber, a 25cm x 25cm square of foam sheet with a hole of 5cm in the center. Exercise

caution and go with the middle of your felt with this hole.

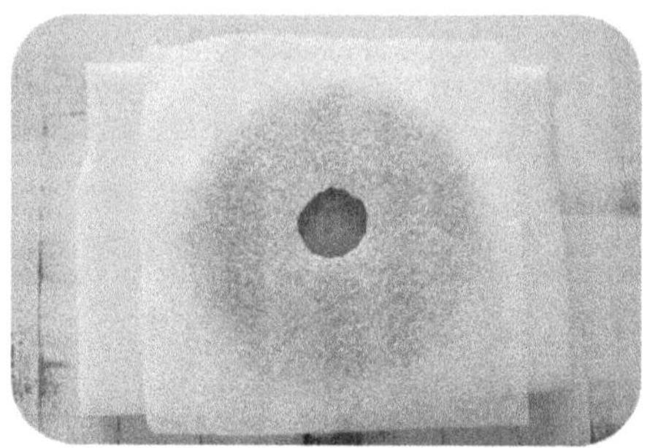

5. Repeat the process on a foam sheet.

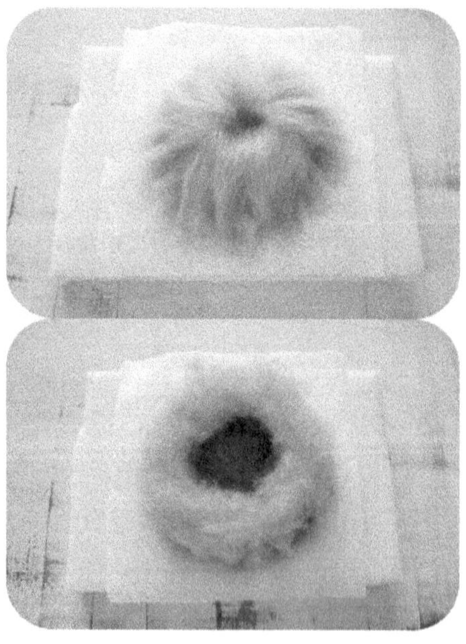

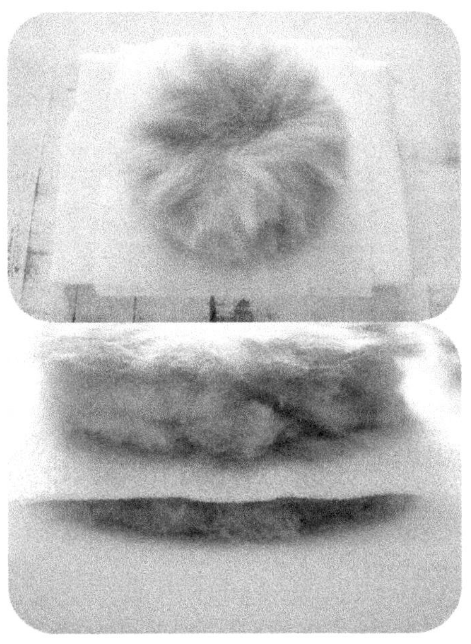

6. Felt with a felting needle to connect the center of Merino layers.

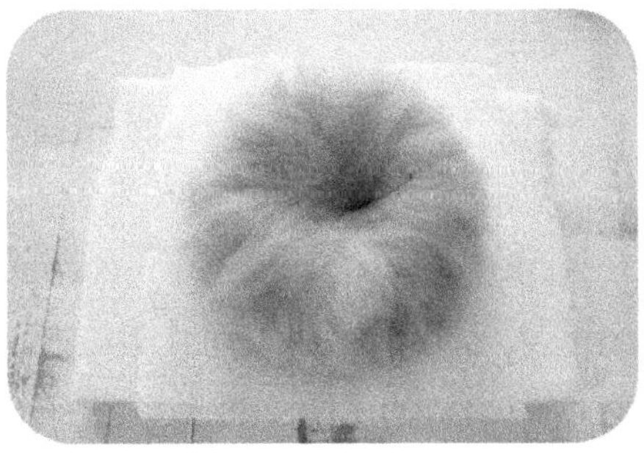

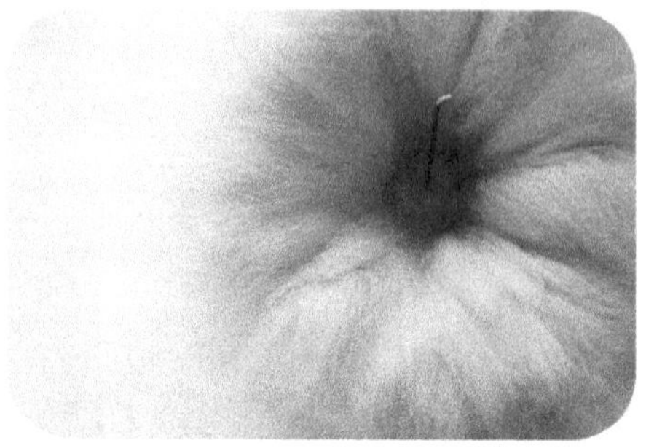

7. Gently take away the foam rubber. Keep your felt
    on the bubble wrap.

8. Wet using soapy water.

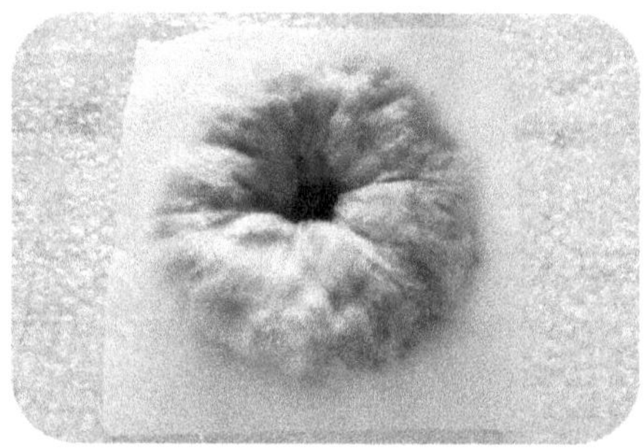

9. Cover the piece with bubble wrap and squeeze
    softly with your hands until the wool is entirely
    wet, both on top and underneath

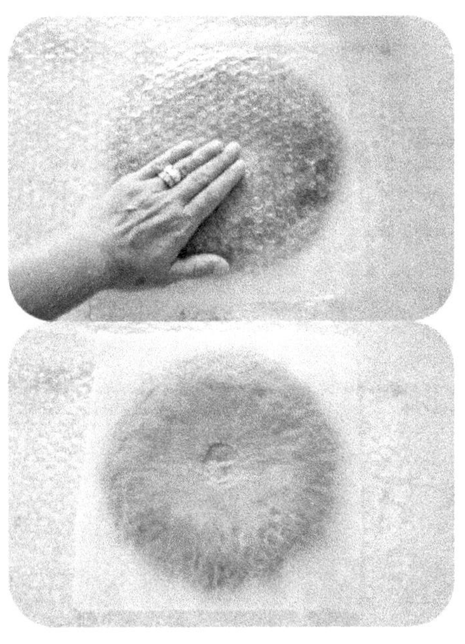

10. Roll the material as a "sushi" piece and start rubbing backward and forward. Repeat the rolling process until your felt has shrunk 30%

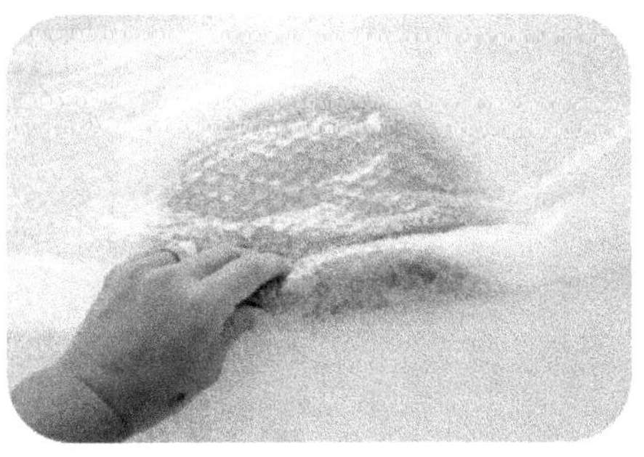

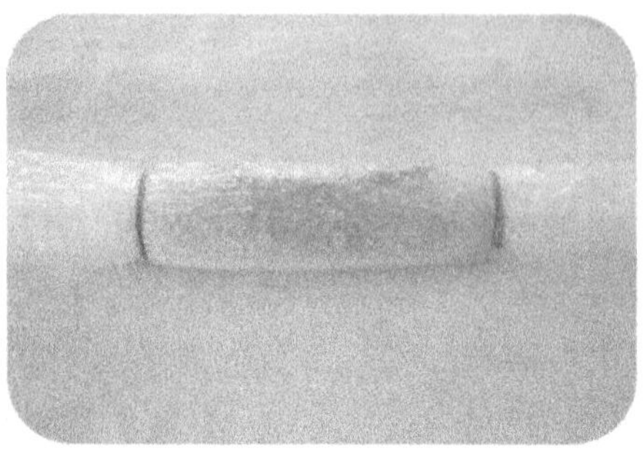

When you are finished rubbing, it will have a diameter of 14cm

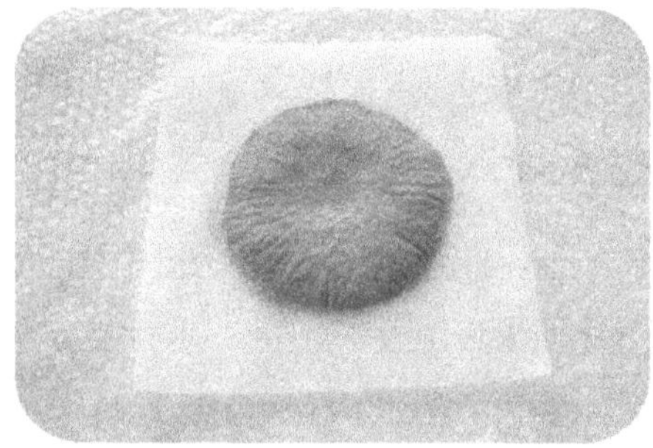

11. Take away the foam sheet and drain the excess water.

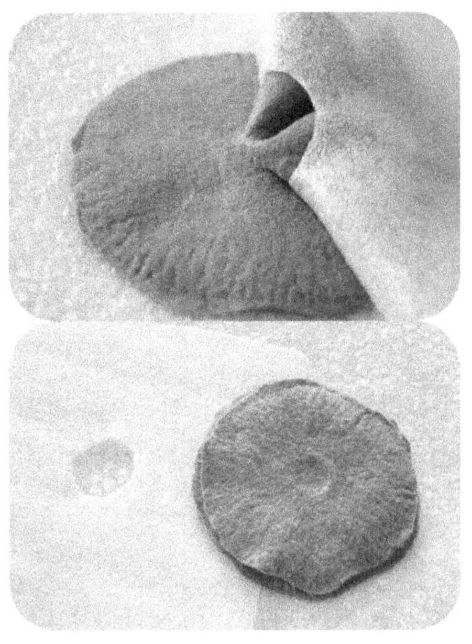

12. Slice the petals. They may have various shapes.

Do not get to the center.

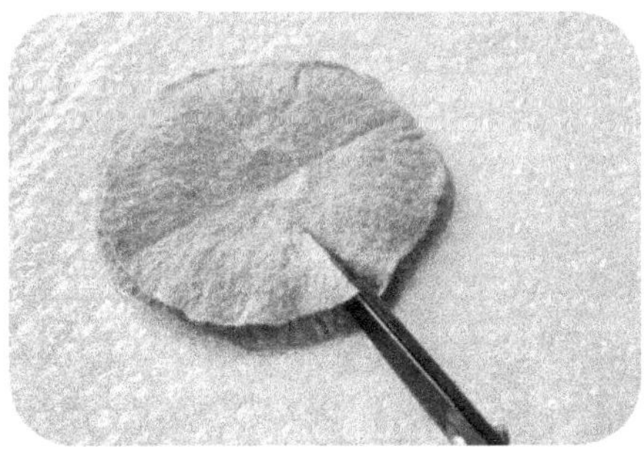

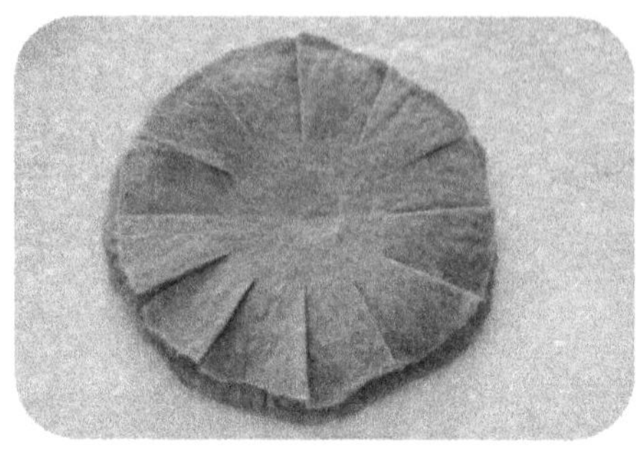

13. After cutting petals from the layers, wet them with soapy water. Rub/ roll the materials like a ball

Once you have cut petals from both layers, wet them again using soapy water and rub/roll the material as if it were a ball.

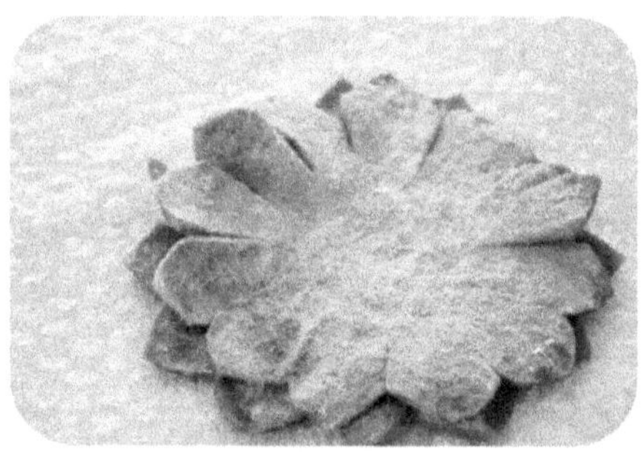

14. Continue to rub until the edges become felted.

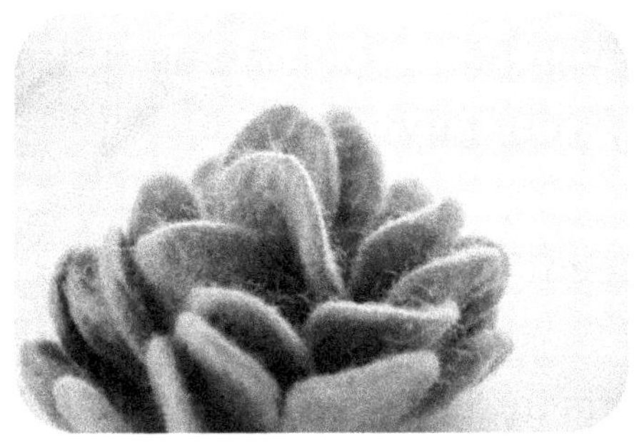

15. You can drain out the excess water as required. Make use of a towel for this process. Then, select a pot you want for your felt fat plants.

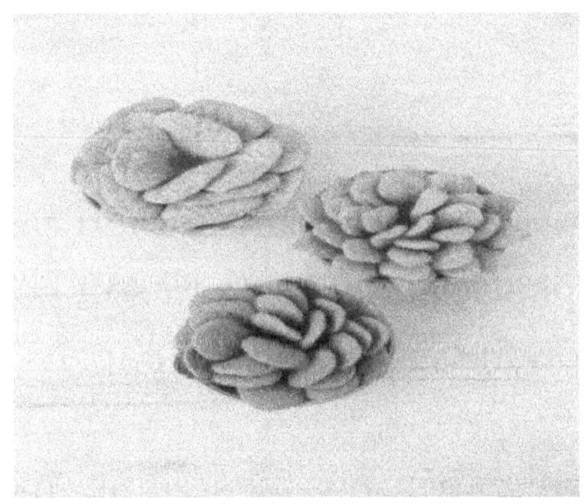

Felted Flowers

This is a perfect project for beginners. You can finish this in less than an hour. You can use this for decoration and to beautify your environment.

Things You Need:

- Wool batts in pink and yellow
- Water-soluble paper
- Coarse (#36) and medium(#38) felting needles
- Felting foam mat
- Scissors
- Soft pencil

Direction

1. Lay the flower template underneath the water-soluble paper, and with your soft pencil, draw the outline on the water-soluble paper.

2. Place the paper on the felting mat. Get some pinch of wool, and lay on the water-soluble paper, extending the sketch of your motif. Ensure that you take only a small amount of wool to

make a small layer. It is better to add more wool than to felt large amount of wool that is hard to felt down, thereby removing the fine look of the flower

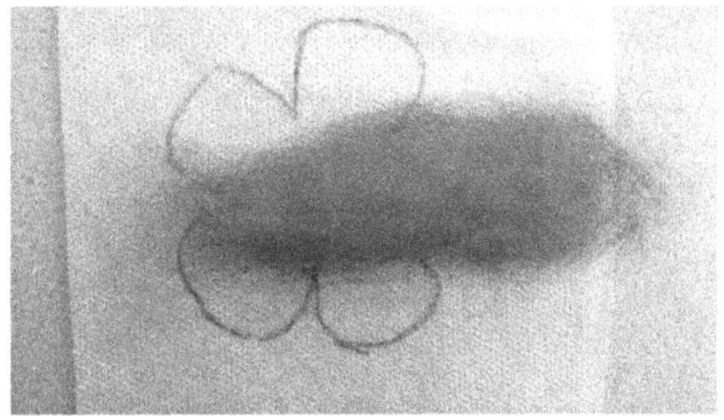

3. Stab with your felting needle in line with your drawn outline under the wool. This will help to pin the outline in position.

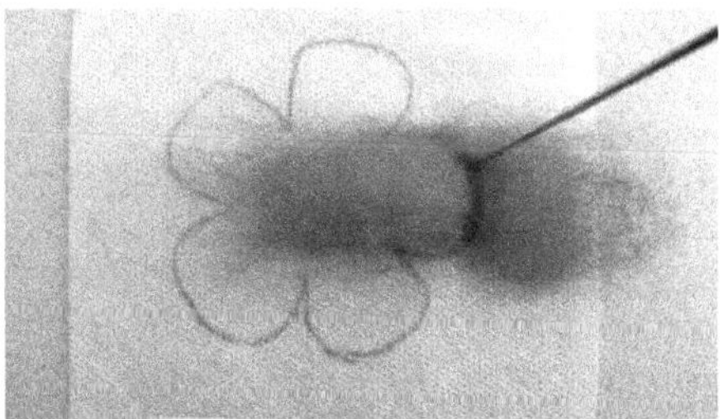

4. Fold fibers outside the outline back into the shape. The pinned fibers will give a clean draft. Felt all through the wool. Also, peel away the paper occasionally from your mat to stop it from being attached.

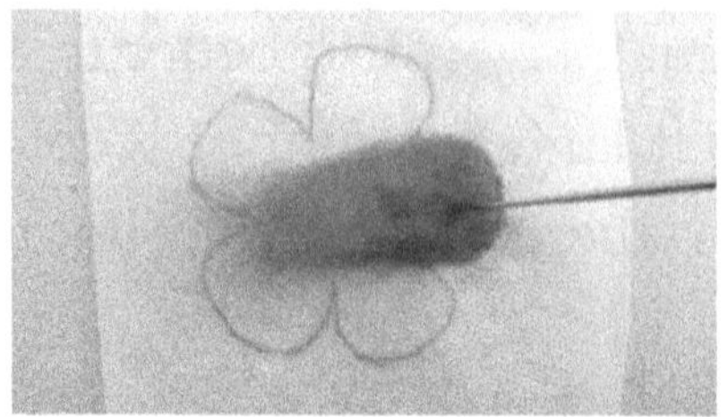

5. Keep working round the shape this way. Now, you can decide to change to the medium needle to offer the flower a smoother finish. Crosscheck by placing it against the light. If you see a thin area, add some wool to ensure a uniform cover.

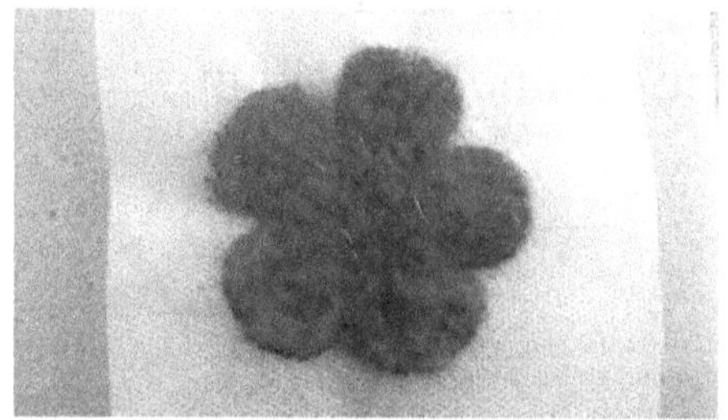

6. Refine the outline of your shape. You can slab the needle for it to be on a lower angle rather than stab straight down with your needle. It works perfectly where you desire a sharp 'V' shape like between the petals

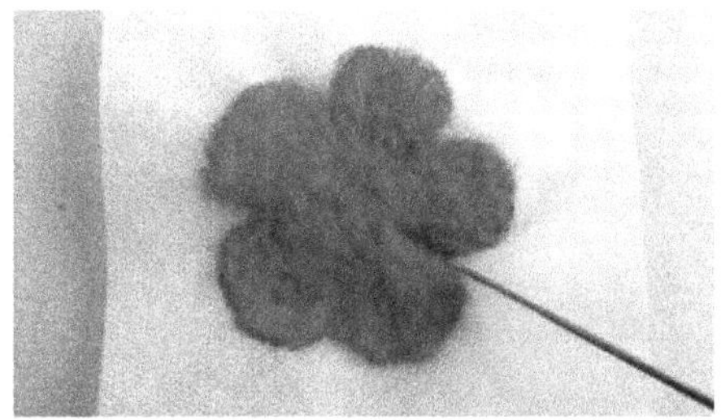

7. Improve the edges of the motif as much as you can before cutting the motif off.

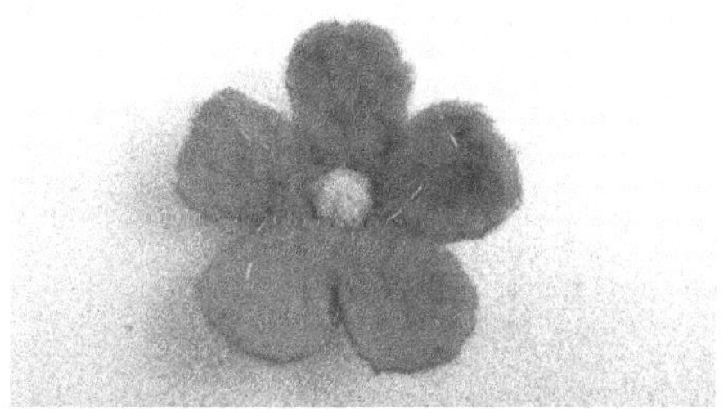

8. Fix a yellow center by felting a ball of pinch wool in the center of the flower. Dissolve the water-soluble paper by soaking it in water for two seconds, and drain the extra water out on a towel. Shape the flower into a cupped position and allow it to dry, and it will remain in that position. You need to smoothen the edges further once it is dry, you can use scissors to do that.

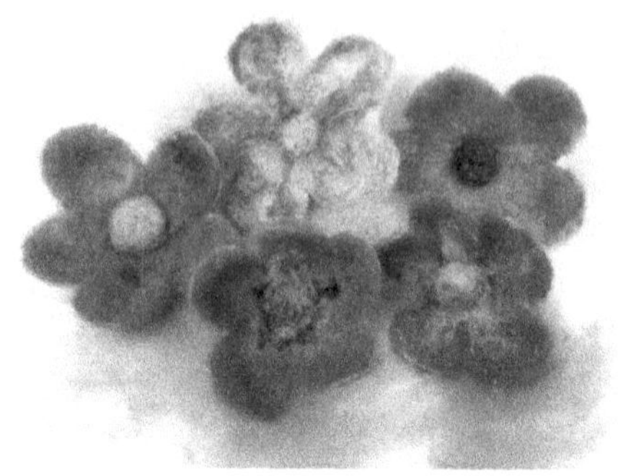

Matryoshka Dolls

Do you want to create a beautiful doll for children? This is the perfect project for you. It will take some time, but you can finish it within a day with enough practice and patience.

Things You Need:

- 5g of flesh-colored wool
- 10g of blue wool
- 5g of yellow wool
- Little amount of white, black, green, red and dark brown wool
- Felting needle
- Foam pad
- Ruler

Direction

Doll Head

1. Measure a 5.1 x 20.3cm (2″ x 8″) piece of flesh-colored wool and fold into a 1 inch (2.5cm) wide ball. Needle the surface to prevent the fibers from unrolling.

2. Needle a channel along the center of the face. This will serve as a guide to position the eyes, nose and help in shaping the face

3. Roll a strand of flesh-colored wool to a ball. Needle in the center of the face for a nose.

4. Needle a strand of wool on each side of the doll's face as the eyes

5. Needle a strand of black wool inside the white eyes

6. Needle a strand of white wool in the black wool of the eye. Also, poke a strand of black wool across the top of the eye as eyelid.

7. Needle a strand of black wool under the nose for the mouth. Fold a strand of red wool slightly and needle underneath the black wool. Needle the

corners of the red wool up so that the doll will appear to be smiling.

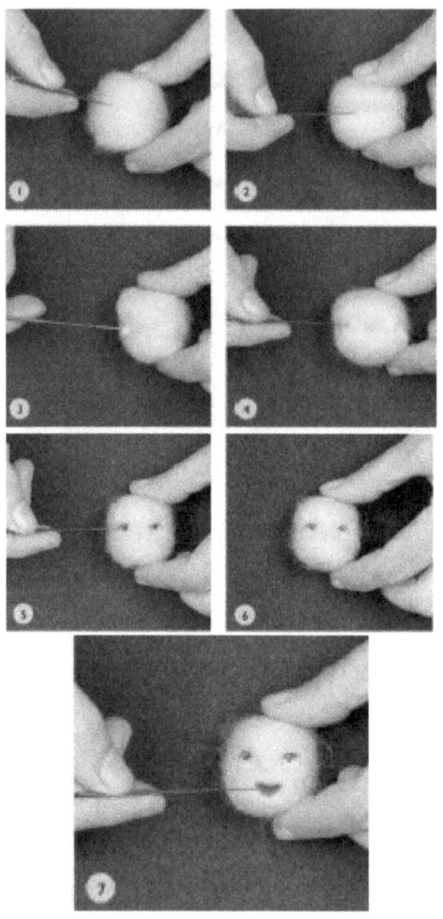

Doll Body

8. Measure a 2″ x 12 in (5.1 x 30.5 cm) piece of blue wool and roll into a 2.5 inches (6.4cm) long barrel shape.

9. Select the part of the body that will serve as the base. Rotate the base side up and needle it flat so that the doll will stand.

10. Needle two 1 x 2 in (2.5 x 5.1 cm) pieces of blue wool flat to create the arms. Roll the length into two and needle. Trim the shape of the arms by lifting the sides and needle them towards the center.

11. Place the arms on both sides of the body and needle all through the corners of the arm and into the body to fix.

12. Needle a strand of flesh-colored wool into a wool and attach it to each arm's wrist to create the hands.

13. Place the head on the body and needle across the edge of the head and into the body to connect.

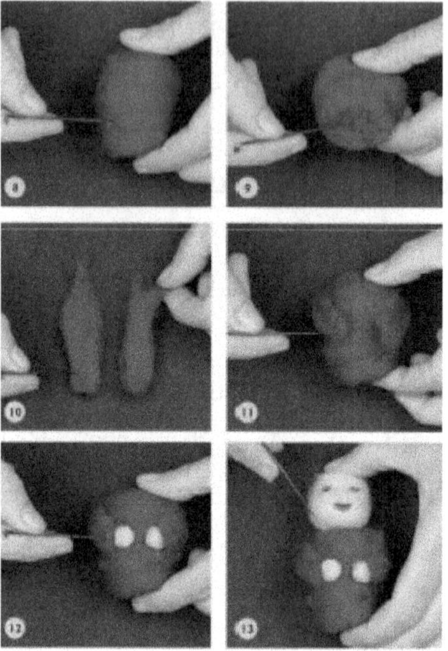

Doll Scarf

14. Measure a 7 x 1 in (17.8 x 2.5cm) piece of yellow wool. Keep the layers of wool apart and lay them out in a triangular shape on the foam pad. Jab the wool flat. Flip the triangle to the other side and needle the other side.

15. Place the scarf over the head of the doll and tie the sides underneath the chin. Needle the corner of the scarf around the head of the doll. Needle round the base edge of the scarf into the body of the doll.

16. Keep needling the scarf till it becomes smooth and shows the shape of the head. Needle the back of the head until it becomes curved.

17. Needle a few strands of dark brown wool across the hairline of the doll.

Details

18. Get creative with the details you want to add to the doll. You can use very small amounts of wool, colorful needle patterns, trims, and decoration on the doll's body and the scarf. Needle some of the bunched-up wool into her hands for a flower. Or, you can needle a heart for the doll to hold.

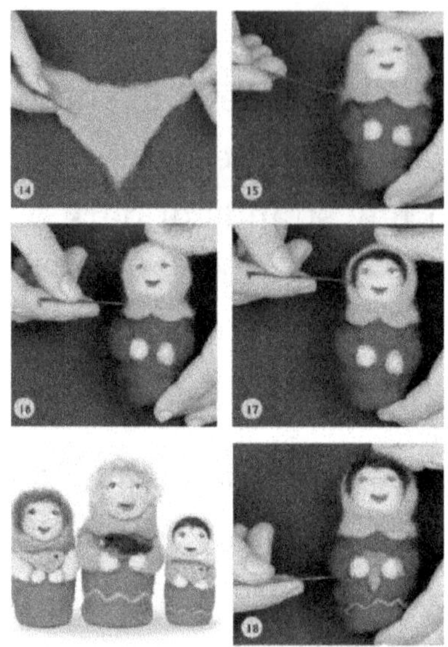

Felted Elephant Pull Toy

This is another favorite for young children that love to pull things along. You can create this project for your children. You can also gift it to new moms.

Things You Need:

- Gray wool (14g)
- Little amount of white and black wool
- Felting needle
- Foam pad
- Ruler

- Four 1 inch (2.5cm) round wooden wheels
- Four ¼ inch (6mm) round wooden beads
- Red acrylic paint
- Small paintbrush
- Craft glue
- 48 inches (122cm) long piece of red satin ribbon
- Two 4 inches (10.2 cm) wooden skewers

Direction

Body

1. Roll a 16 x 2 ½ inches (40.6 x 6.4cm) piece of gray wool tightly into a 4″ x 2″ (10.2 x 5.1 cm) tube shape. Needle the surface to help the surface to hold.

Head

2. Roll a 16 inches (40.6 cm) piece of gray wool into a 2 inches (5.1 cm) round ball and needle the surface to keep the ball from unrolling.

3. Keep the head on one side of the body. Needle the fibers from the head into the body to

connect. Put extra wool round the neck area and needle to form a smooth attachment.

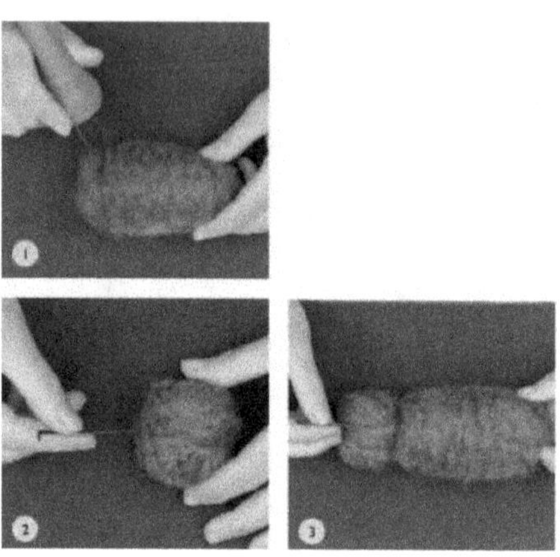

Trunk

4. Roll a 12 x 1 in (30.5 x 2.5 cm) piece of gray wool into 3 ½ in (8.9 cm) long trunk with a felting needle. Leave the fibers loose at an end to connect the trunk to the head.

5. Place the loose fibers of the trunk on the front of the elephant's head and needle to attach. Cover the area of attachment using a layer of fibers and fiber across the trunk to smoothen it.

6. Needle a piece of gray wool into an oval shape and connect it under the trunk as a chin.

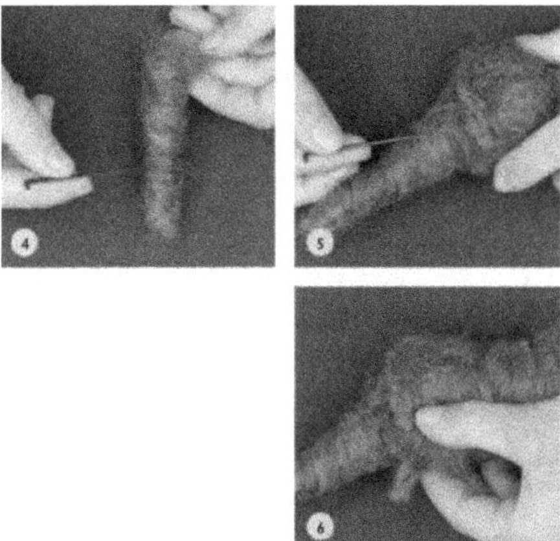

Legs

7. With the needle, tightly roll a 9 x 2 in (22.9 x 5.1 cm) piece of gray wool into a 3 in (7.6 cm) long leg. Leave the fibers loose at one side and needle the fibers at the other end to make a flat foot.

8. Create three more legs the same way.

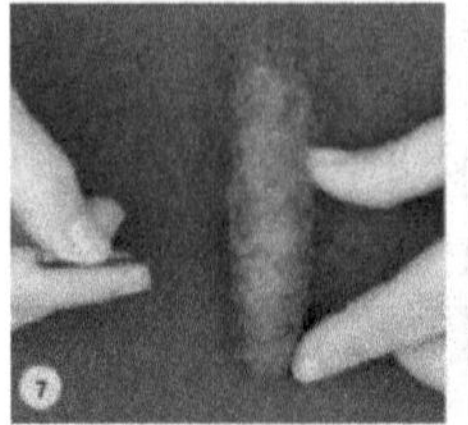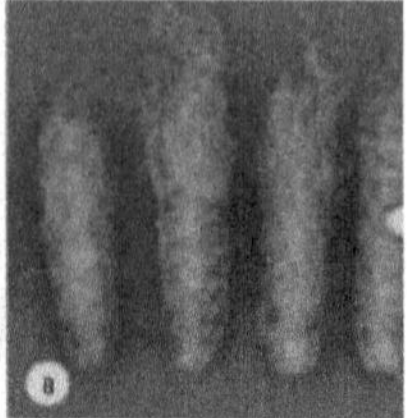

Attach the Body to the Head

9. Place the loose fibers of the legs on the side of the elephant's body and needle to attach.

10. Fix a layer of gray wool round the area of attachment so that the elephant can stand strong on its legs. Fill the area with wool and needle until it becomes smooth.

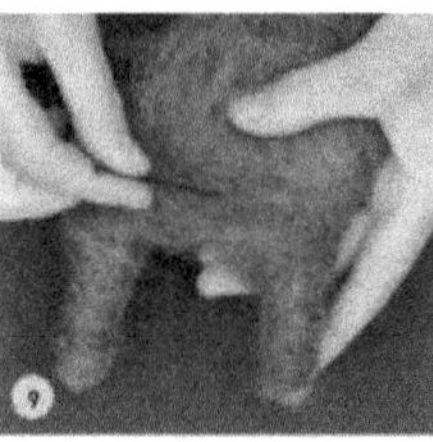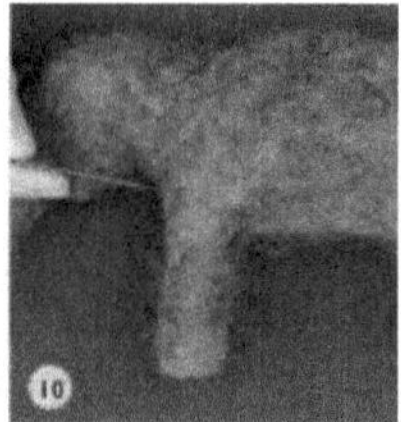

Ears

11. Needle felt a 2 in (5.1 cm) piece of gray wool to a flat oval shape. Lift the wool off the foam pad and needle the back. Form the ear by lifting the fibers from the edge of the ear towards the

middle. Leave the fibers loose at one edge to help connect the ear to the head. Create two ears.

12. Place the ears on either side of the head and needle the ears' loose fibers into the head to connect.
13. Push the ears towards the back of the head and needle inside the ear to form a secure attachment.

14. Needle a strand of white wool into the middle part of each ear.

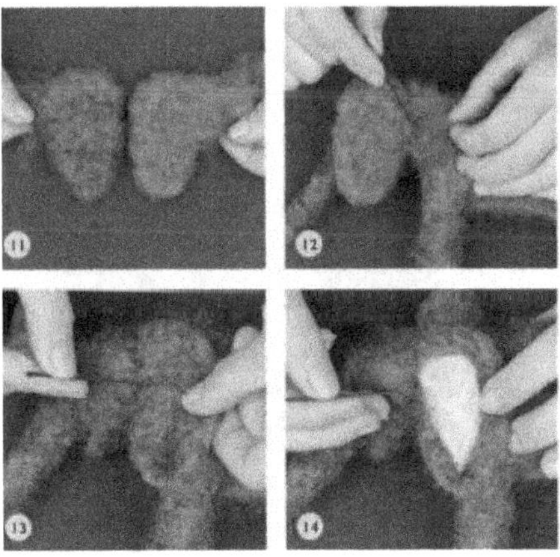

Eyes

15. Needle felt a little strand of white wool into a circle on both sides of the elephant's head. Felt a smaller black circle within the white.

16. Needle a tiny white speck in the black circle.

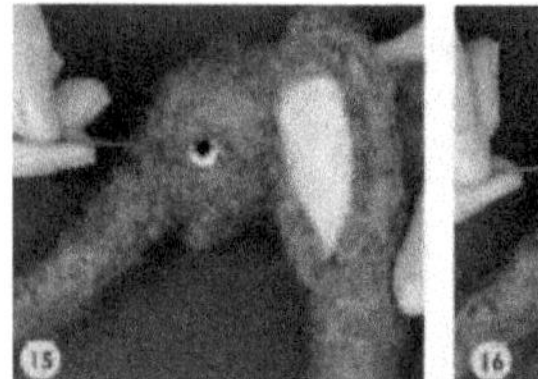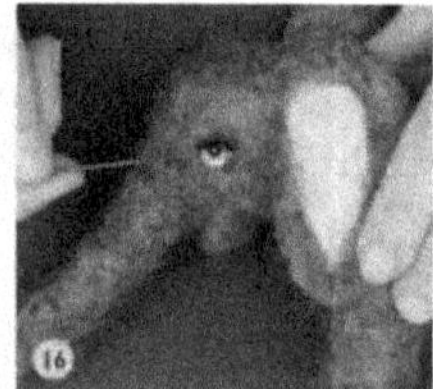

Tail

17. Roll a 3 in (7.6 cm) piece of gray wool into a long, thin shape. Allow the fibers to remain loose at an end and attach the tail to the back of the elephant.

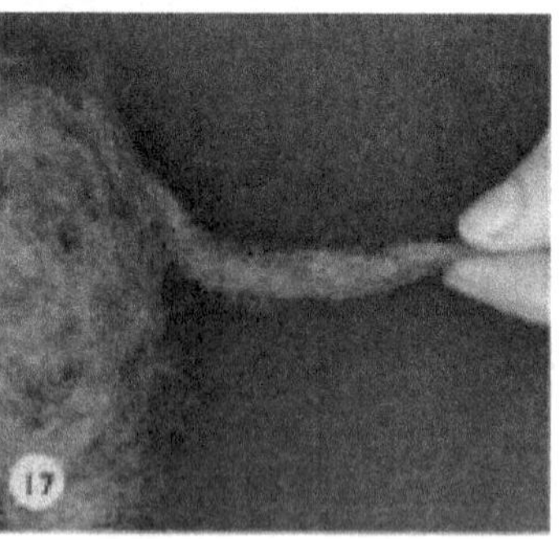

Pull Frame

18. Paint the beads, wooden skewers, and wheels with red acrylic paint and allow the parts to dry overnight.

19. Twist the pointed end of the skewer gently into the bottom part of the elephant's leg. Twist the skewer all through the opposite leg and out. Do the same with the back leg and other wooden skewers.

20. Keep the wooden wheels on the end of the skewers. You can also twist the wheels on to make them fit. Paste the wooden beads on the end of the skewer so that the wheels will roll freely and not slide off.

21. Tie the red ribbon on the front skewer and the elephant becomes ready to roll.

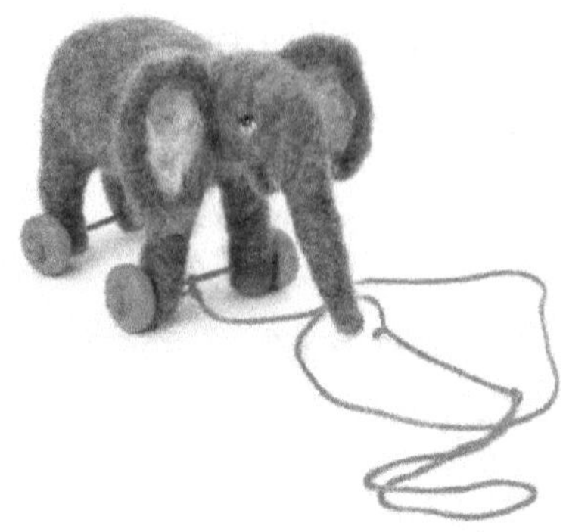

Felted Teddy Bear

This is an amazing project to work on. Wool is soft to the touch and makes this project a snuggly delight. It is also perfect for children.

Let's start creating.

Materials You Will Need:

- 14g of gold wool
- Little amount of white and dark brown wool
- Felting needle
- Foam pad
- Ruler

Direction

Body

1. Roll an 18 x 14 in (45.7 x 10.2 cm) piece of gold wool tightly into a 5 x 4 in (12.7 x 10.2 cm) egg shape. Felt to help in holding the shape and keep the fibers from unrolling.

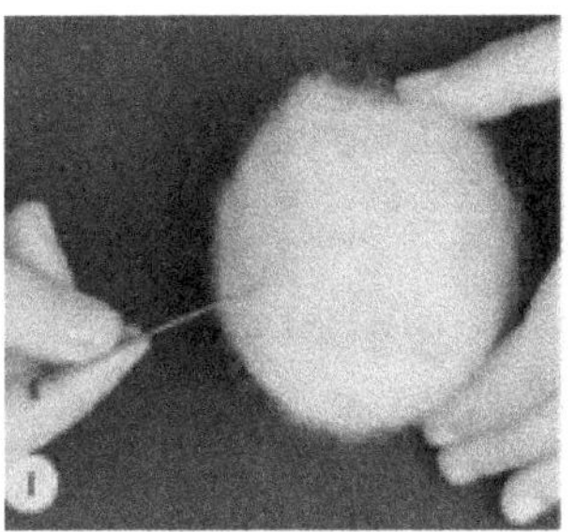

Head

2. Roll a 12 x 2 in (30.5 x 5.1 cm) piece of gold wool into a 3 in (7.6 cm) round ball and needle to hold the shape.

3. Place the head on top of the body and needle to connect.

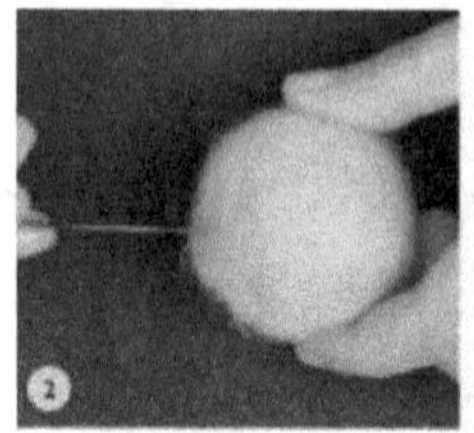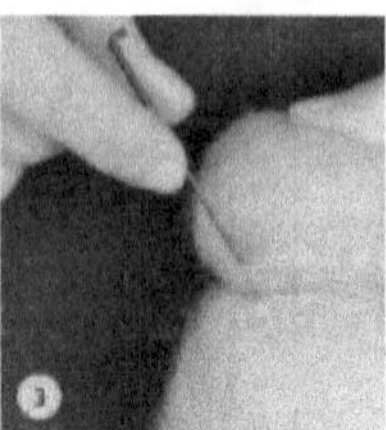

Legs and Arms

4. Roll a 12 x 2 in (30.5 x 5.1 cm) piece of gold wool into a 4 in (10.2cm) long tube shape. Leave the fibers loose at one end.

5. Needle an indentation at the instep to help in shaping the foot.

6. Needle a grove at the back of the knee on the leg.

7. Repeat the steps to create a second leg.

8. The arms will be similarly created to the legs. Roll a 10 x 1 in (25.4 x 2.5 cm) piece of gold wool to a 3 ½ inches (8.9cm) long tube shape. Allow the fibers to be loose at one end to help attach the arms to the body.

9. Repeat the steps to create a second arm.

10. Place the legs on either side of the bear's body and needle to attach.

11. The legs of the bear are placed so that the bear can sit up.

12. Position the arms on the bear's body, just above the legs, and needle to attach.
13. Ensure that the arms and legs are attached securely and uniformly spaced.
14. Wrap another layer of wool around the attachment area between the legs and body and needle until it becomes smooth.
15. Wrap an extra layer of wool round the arms, head, and neck area. Needle so that the areas of attachment is smooth.
16. Add some extra wool from the neck up and around the head. Needle the wool smooth.

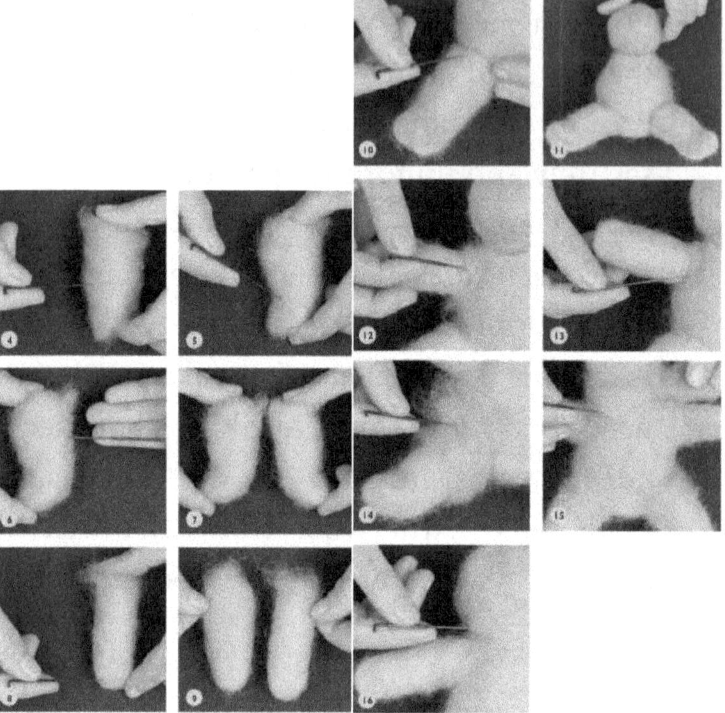

Ears

17. Needle 2 wisps of gold wool into ¼ in (1.9 cm) round circles. Allow the fibers to remain loose at the end to help to attach the ears to the head

18. Place the ears on either side of the bear head and needle to fix.

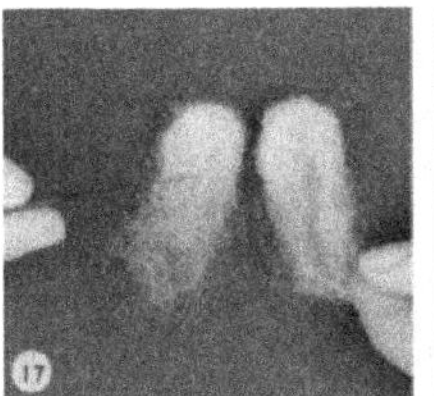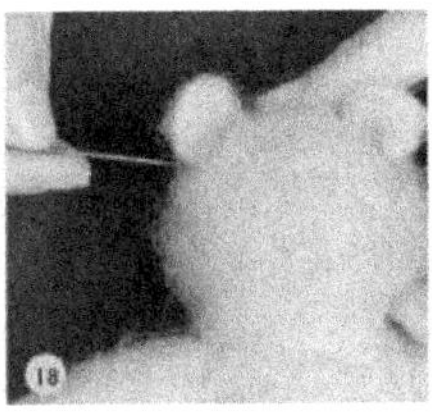

Face Details

19. Roll a 3 in (7.6 cm) piece of gold wool into a ¼ in (1.9 cm) ball and needle it to the front of the bear's face for a snout.
20. Needle a small ½ inch (1.3 cm) disc of gold wool underneath the snout for a mouth.
21. Needle a strand of dark brown wool on the tip of the snout for a nose. Needle a line of dark brown wool under the nose.
22. Needle 2 circles of white wool on the face of the bear for the eyes.
23. Needle a smaller circle of dark brown wool inside each white circle.
24. Needle a speck of white wool inside of each dark brown circle.
25. Layer some gold wool on the bear's tummy and needle it smooth and round.

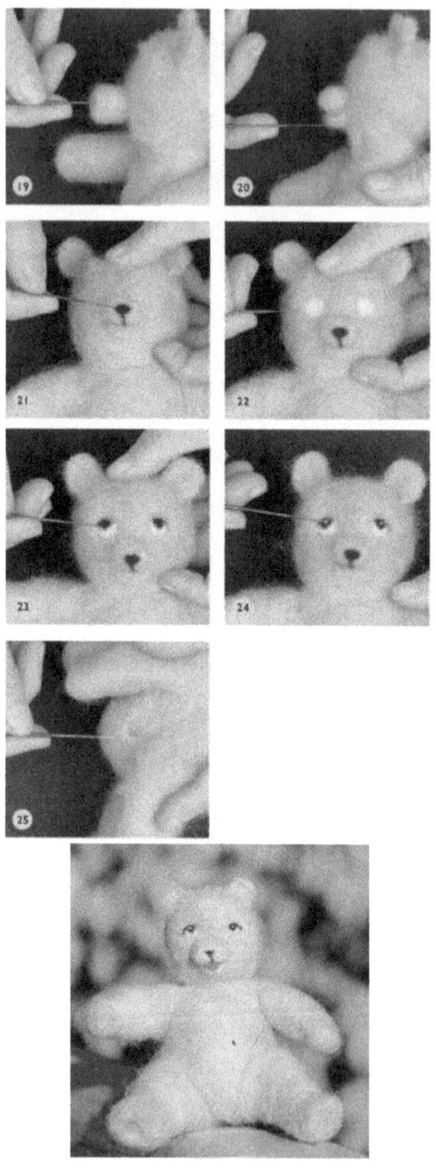

181

Dala Horse

This is another 3-dimensional animal project that you can use as a toy. It takes time and some patience, but you will come out successful if you try.

I am rooting for you!

Things You Need:

- 14g of red wool
- Little amount of white, green, orange and yellow wool
- Darning needle
- Soap
- Spray bottle
- Warm water
- Wooden skewer
- Felting needle
- Foam pad
- Ruler
- Towel

Direction

Body

1. Measure an 8 x 2 in (20.3 x 5.1cm) piece of red wool and tightly roll into a 3 x 1 in (7.6 x 2.5 cm) barrel shape.
2. Fix another layer of wool and needle the surface to help the fiber from unrolling.

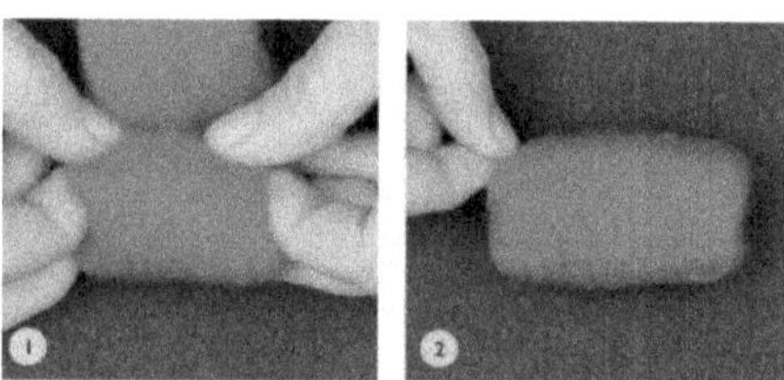

Neck/Head

3. Measure a 6 x 2 in (15.2 x 5.1 cm) piece of red wool and roll into a 1 ½ in (3.8 cm) cone. Needle the surface all through to secure the fibers in place.

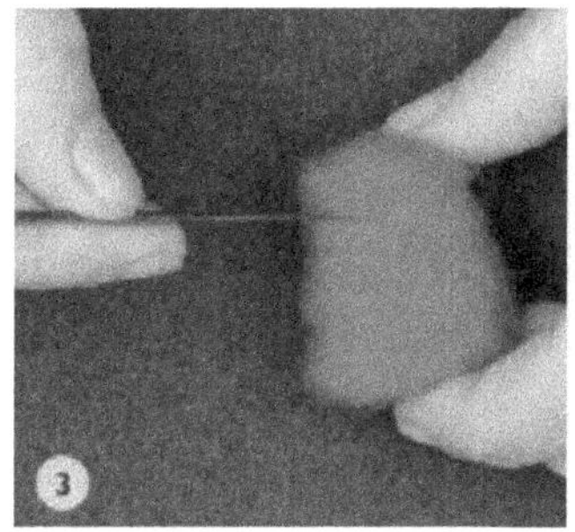

Muzzle

4. Needle a 4 x 1 in (10.2 x 2.5 cm) piece of red wool into a 1 x 1 ½ in (2.5 x 1.3 cm) cone.

5. Place the muzzle on the head/neck piece and needle all across the muzzle's edge into the head to attach.

6. Protect the area of attachment with the strand of red wool to help smoothen any lines. Needle to help in forming a strong attachment.

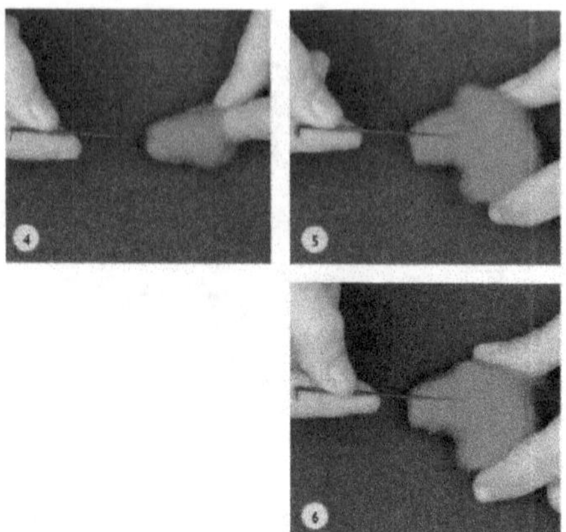

Ears

7. Stab the felting needle on the top of the horse's head and pull the wool up to form the ears gently.

8. Needle around the ears to help in forming the shape.

9. Place the head and neck on the body and needle all around the base of the neck into the body to attach.

10. Needle a strand of red wool around the area of attachment so that it becomes smooth.

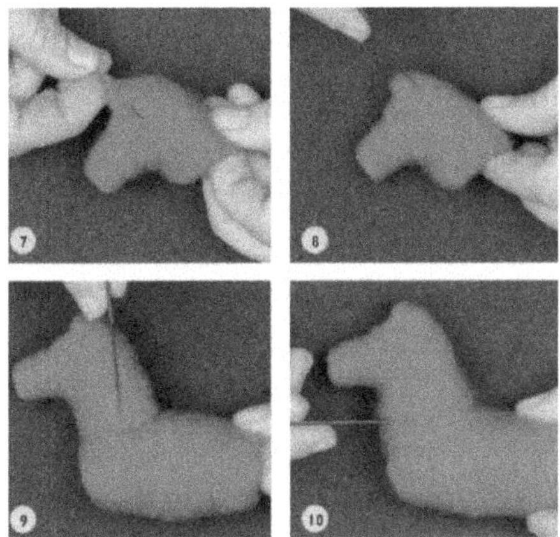

Legs

11. Roll a 6 x 1 in (15.2 x 2.5 cm) piece of red wool into a 2 in (5.1 cm) long leg shape.
12. Make three more legs.
13. Place a leg on one side of the horse's body and needle to attach.
14. Fix the other three legs, then add some more red wool around the area of attachment to improve the legs' strength. Needle the wool to smoothen the surface.
15. Fill a small spray bottle with warm, soapy water. Place a towel underneath the horse and lightly spray all over the body. Massage the wet, soapy wool until a skin is formed on the surface. Pat the

surface dry with the towel and allow the horse to dry before continuing to the next steps.

16. When the horse becomes dry, ensure that the legs are uniform and needle to make any necessary body shape adjustments.

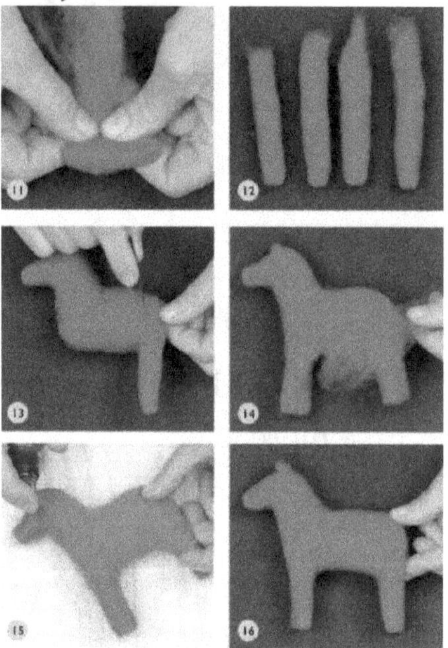

Details

17. Use the smallest amount of merino wool to needle the design on the surface.

18. Use white merino to make a flower-shaped saddle and reins.

19. Outline the white wool with green merino wool.
Needle orange wool into the middle of each white
circle and in the flower's center on the horse's
back.

20. Needle some yellow wool on the back of the
horse's neck to make a mane. Outline the yellow
wool with green wool.

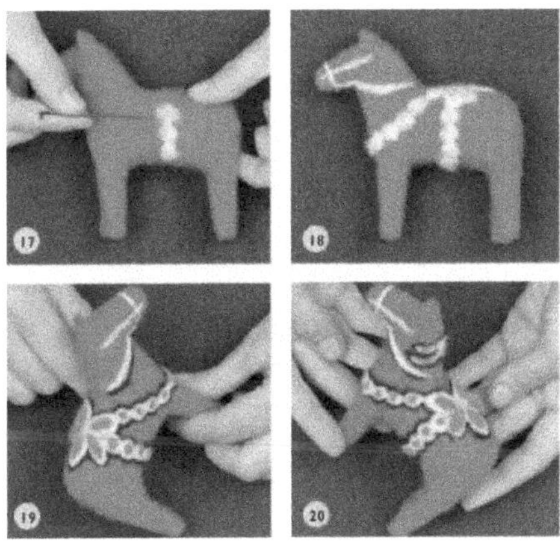

The end... almost!

Hey! We've made it to the final chapter of this book, and I hope you've enjoyed it so far.

If you have not done so yet, I would be incredibly thankful if you could take just a minute to leave a quick review on Amazon

Reviews are not easy to come by, and as an independent author with a little marketing budget, I rely on you, my readers, to leave a short review on Amazon.

Even if it is just a sentence or two!

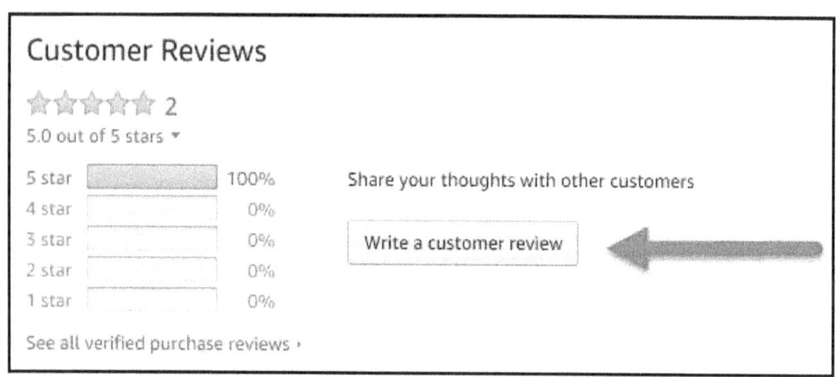

So if you really enjoyed this book, please...

>> Click here to leave a brief review on Amazon.

I truly appreciate your effort to leave your review, as it truly makes a huge difference.

Chapter 6

Frequently Asked Questions on Needle Felting

This chapter will answer all your questions and ease every confusion you have concerning needle felting. If you have encountered any difficulty in your needle felting, this chapter will provide clarity to them.

What type of needles are used for needle felting?

The needles used for needle felting are usually very thin needles that are often fitted in holders that allow the users to use two or more needles simultaneously to sculpt objects and shapes. The thinner needle is useful for details, while the multiple needles are paired together and operated for more significant areas to form the object's foundation.

What is the best needle I should use for needle felting?

It would be best if you use different types of needles on different gauges. A lot of kits also use more than a needle. You can also buy packs of the needle at affordable prices because you will end up breaking some. However, purchasing a 38-gauge needle is an excellent choice for a beginner. Also, go for needles with more grooves that will allow you to felt more efficiently but may not be needed when working on details.

What are the uses of needle felting?

Needle felting can be used for creating different crafts, ranging from 2D objects to 3D objects. You can use it for both industrial and individual skills.

What are the materials I need for needle felting?

It would be best if you had a felting needle, wool, and felting cushion. These items are cheap. Immediately you get these supplies; you can start your felting journey. However, refer to the section of this book on Essential Tools and Materials Needed for more details.

How do I know that I am using the right needle?

The general rule is that you need to use a 36-38 gauge for the coarsest fibers, 38 gauge for medium (best multi-purpose), and 40 or even 42 gauge for fine fibers. Nevertheless, you might use all of them to some degree throughout a project – a 38 gauge will felt faster than 40, but it leaves bigger holes. Even though your piece was not completed with fine fibers, a 40 will help you smoothen things out.

How can I earn from needle felting?

There are several ways you can earn from needle felting, and they include:

- Selling your crafts: You can sell your felted objects in various places, both online and offline.
- Creating and selling your kits for others to make things: You can design and create kits for people to buy.
- Work on Commission: Instead of creating lots of things, you can get commissioned work. This way, you will know that you will sell the item and not spend time on things that may not sell or may not sell for a while.
- Online Tutorials: You can create online courses that will give people the information that they need concerning needle felting at a reasonable price.

- Books or Ebooks: You can write ebooks on needle felting and enlighten people on the subject at a price.
- Offline Courses: You can also organize and run the course locally. From there, you can sell wool, books, and equipment to your students.

What is the best method of learning needle felting?

The best way to learn needle felting is to have a go at it. Like wet felting, you will discover the methods that are best for you. The technique is easy – you jab the barbed felting needle through the wool until it gradually entangles together by drawing fibers from below back up via the fibers on top. With time, you will create simple beads and patterns.

Must I use a base material?

You can felt wool to any shape you desire by needling it on a foam pad or a special needle felting brush.

Which is better, wool top or carded wool?

There are no right or wrong answers, and it depends on the wool you are using, what you are producing, and your personal preference. However, you should not begin your needle felting journey with Merino wool, as it is not just suitable. It is too delicate and does not easily felt. It also makes the whole project a hard one to crack.

Can I needle felt on wet-felt?

You can needle-felt on wet-felted materials to add details.

Why does my needle break easily?

Felting needles can break faster if you bend your needle during felting. Continue to poke the needle straight into the wool and draw it straight out at the same angle. Work with a foam pad or special needle felting brush so that the needle will not break.

What type of projects do you, wet felt, or needle felt?

Needle felting can be used for wool paintings, sculptures, disguising mistakes for wet felted projects, mending wet felt projects, and decorative purposes.

Wet felting is used to make clothes and bags or other substantial decorative items. When it is fulled, the felt can be gently washed by hand in warm water. It will not do any harm to the felt because it is already merged in water and soap.

Where can I sell my needle felted crafts?

You can sell on Etsy, a great online marketplace mainly made for handmade, custom, and vintage goods. You can list your needle felted projects and start your own Etsy store. The payments are deposited straight to your bank account, and it is the simplest means to get your products before your customers.

Also, you need to put yourself out there on social media. Take control of Facebook, Instagram, and Pinterest. Use those platforms to share your love for crafting.

You can also use Youtube to pass your message across and build your brand. Also, build an online community that you can share your craft with. Please get to know other felters and share your crafts with them. It will help to boost your visibility, influence, and income.

Do I need a website to sell my felting projects?

If you want to thrive as a needle felter, you need your website as a needle felter. It should not be a freebie setups or a general site, but a personal website through WordPress and a domain name. A website is not difficult to set up these days. With some learning, you can do it. A website helps you to brand yourself and your business and serves as your online real estate. You can also use your website to brand yourself as an authority in needle felting.

Must I use the coarsest wool there is?

No, you don't have to. It would be best if you used something that has the consistency of fiberfill and less like silk.

Does it matter whether it is roving or batting?

No, they are both okay for needle felting. I have worked with both of them and have not experienced any issue with either of them. However, I prefer roving for wool painting because it gives a defined line that virtually gives it the same effect as brush strikes. When you are creating a 3D felted piece, batting is better to use, especially if you do not want any lines showing.

What is the use of wire armature?

A wire armature can be used for 3D animals to help the process and provide support, around which a needle felted body and coat can be added.

What are needle-felting or embellishment machines?

Needle-felting or embellishment machines are popular for art or craft felters. It works in a similar way to a sewing machine. Needle felting machines have several needles that punch fibers together as the user punches fibers through a very similar way of feeding a sewing machine. The embellishment machine lets the user make a unique mix of fibers and designs.

What is the best wool for long animal fur?

You can choose anyone that works, including Merino. Herdwick sheep naturally have a long coat of Herdwick, but Merino and Corriedale are suitable for dogs and cats.

Can I use plant fibers for needle felting?

They are not too suitable for three-dimensional projects but are ideal for adding luster, interest, and color to many projects. You can use plant fiber, but it is a big struggle and a chore, and the result will not be nearly as good as wool. Like bamboo, plant fibers do not felt well because they are smoother; wool has tiny scales that interlock when rubbed, agitated, or compressed with a felting needle. From former experiences and others' experiences, vegetable fibers are not suitable alone, although they can be mixed with wool or used on finished wool projects. Bamboo and silk tops can bring a lovely luxurious texture, sheen, and contrast to your project. You can use silk in needle felted crafts, pumpkins, hats, and gnome beads.

Can I over felt wool?

Yes! The more you needle felt, the more you break down the wool fibers. When you over felt, by poking the wool in the same spot for too long, the fibers will break down eventually and begin to go soft. When this happens, it is best to start with fresh wool.

What is the difference between wool tops and carded wool?

They are both the same wool with separate processes. Wool tops are produced in long lengths, mainly the thickness of your wrist, quite heavy with the fibers brushed in the same direction. Carded wool fibers are shorted and brushed in different directions, giving rise to loftier wool.

Can I needle felt every wool?

No!

However, most wool can be wet felted or incorporated into wet felting.

What is core wool?

Core wool signifies different things to different people, and that is where most of the confusion lies. It just means what you use for the center or bulk of your project, and it can be any medium/coarse wool if your top layer is a different color or uses a fine wool, Merino, Corriedale, or similar. Core wool can be used to needle felt your basic shape and then covered with dyed wool.

However, for many projects, it isn't necessary. Different core wool is beneficial when you create life-sized animals or use a more expensive dyed wool as your top color for birds, realistic animals, Christmas baubles, fruit, dragons, Easter eggs, gnome hats, among others. These projects would be much easier to needle felt with a core of coarse wool and then covered with a top layer of bright Shetland, Corriedale, or Merino.

Can I buy vegetarian wool?

Yes, you can, and the availability is increasing. Vegetarian wool, also called slaughter-free wool, means that when the animal dies, it is not sent to slaughter and does not end up in the food chain.

What do I do when my project does not mirror what I am trying to make?

Never fret. Continue. Your project will not resemble anything close to what you are trying to create till you get at least ¾ of the way through. Continue to punch with great determination, and as you continue, they will all come together at the end. The feeling that you are wasting your time always comes with being a beginner. As you continue to shape and add details, you will get the result that you desire. You can also step out of it for some time and bring fresh ideas on how to improve it. You can also search the internet for fresh ideas. Check Pinterest. It is the world's biggest free crafting magazine. Sometimes, you might finish and still not get the vision you had in mind. Please don't stress yourself over it. Continue to improve your craft until you barely make mistakes.

What type of work surface should I use for needle felting?

Felting needles are very sharp and fragile; therefore, you need a firm and resilient work pad to hold all the stabbings. If your surface is not resilient enough, you can break the needle. You can use a folded towel, old couch cushions, pillows, foam gardens kneelers.

What are the precautionary measures I should observe while using felting needles?

- Always keep your eyes on the needle as you felt. The ends of the felting needles are sharp, and you can harm yourself.

- Hold the needle vertically to your working surface to avoid needle breakage. The needle felts well when you hold it vertically.
- Keep the needles back into the plastic sleeves and bag they came in after use.
- Do not keep your felting needles on wet wool. It could lead to rusting.
- Work on a strong table that has good lighting. Curling up on a couch with wool and sharp felting needles can be dangerous.
- For your work surface, use a felting pad to work. You might be tempted to hold your project in your hand during needle felting. However, it can lead to needle breakage and injury. It is better to allow the dense poly foam to absorb the felting needle and keep the project stable and bounce-free. Also, avoid thick upholstery because the upholstery makes your work bouncy and leads to needle breakage and accident. Focusing on bouncing projects can give you weary eyes.

Conclusion

Wow!

We have gotten to the end of this fantastic book. If you read this book to this point, I say congratulations; you are the kind of person that succeeds.

This book has provided you with detailed information on needle felting and exposed you to a step-by-step guide on carrying out needle felting. You have also learned how to create over 15 projects ranging from simple buttons to Christmas decorations, 3D animal projects, and toys of several sizes and colors.

Needle felting is an amazingly easy craft that only requires some wool, felting needle, and foam at the barest minimum. This craft is best for anyone that loves fiber arts or making miniature. You can either be simple or detailed as you desire in your creations. By poking the needles repeatedly into the wool, the fibers will become dense, helping you form various shapes. You can choose from different options for wool, but most felters prefer medium-coarse wool.

However, be warned! Needle felting can be addictive and can make you forgo your daily activities. Therefore, you need to be careful. Remember not to get sucked into it. Make out time for other essential activities.

You will not become an expert overnight. Be ready to make a LOT of mistakes and learn from them. Don't allow your mistakes to stop you from moving forward. If you continue, you will get to the point where you will hardly make any mistake. Take the bull by the horn and start needle felting today. Do not be afraid. Go easy on yourself. You can do it.

Also, exercise the necessary precautionary measures while felting. Always use your felting pad, and watch your movement. Please, don't stab yourself, and take things slowly. You can increase your speed as you become better.

Protect your crafts from your pets. Pets love wool and would always go for them. Therefore, keep them out of the way of your pets.

I also want you to know that needle felting can bring in some good cash beyond making crafts and 3D animal projects for fun, but only if you remain consistent with the craft and become good at it. Join felting communities to create valuable connections, sell on Etsy, Amazon, eBay, and social media channels like Facebook and Instagram. Build an authority website, share your knowledge online, and who knows, you just might make a good living off your crafts.

Also, try out new projects. Do not limit yourself to a similar kind of project. Remember that with needle felting, you can create almost any object that you want. Be wild with your imagination.

It is my honor to usher you on this journey, and I am sincerely rooting for you.

So, start crafting awesome designs with felting needles TODAY!